The Essential
Great Chicago Fire

William Pack

The Essential Great Chicago Fire

Copyright © 2014 by William Pack

williampack.com

ISBN 13: 978-1512387599
ISBN 10: 1512387592

Printed in USA

For the uncountable chances
that continue to inspire
me daily.

Table of Contents

Acknowledgements

First, I must remind you that this book is the product of secondary sources. Robert Cromie, Richard F. Bales, Jim Murphy, and Donald L. Miller did the primary research and all of them wrote fine books on the fire or, in the case of Donald L. Miller, a fine book on the history of Chicago. Those books are the basis for my work and are listed in the bibliography.

I need to thank Elaine Cassell for being my initial reader and editor and for her great advice and patient corrections. This book simple would not exist without her. Any mistakes in this manuscript are entirely the fault of the stubborn author.

All images are from the author's collection unless otherwise noted.

Thank you for supporting books printed on actual paper!

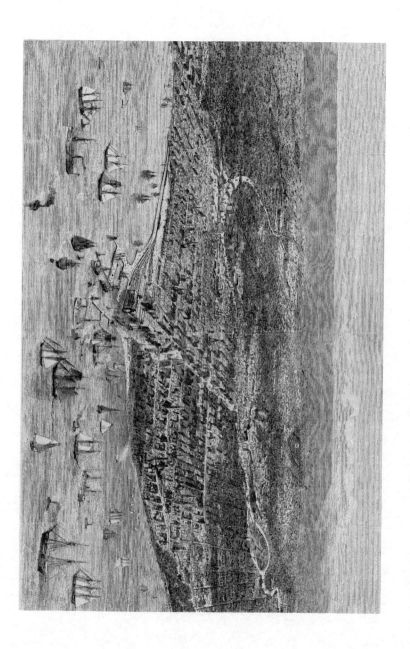

Introduction

All my life I have lived in a world of stories. At a very young age, my Great Aunt Bernice, a great teller of tales, regaled me with all sorts of true and not-so-true stories. I spent my childhood at 49th and Damen, on the Southwest side of Chicago. At eight years old, I discovered the Back of the Yards branch of the Chicago Public Library. I was hooked.

A couple times a week, I would walk the half mile with my little red wagon and fill it with books. (Almost 40 years later, I still have that wagon. A couple of the books, too, but that is beside the point.) The librarians knew me and let me have free rein. I read at a high level and borrowed books way over what a young child should. I distinctly remember a book about undersea photography, something I had no expectation of doing. I think I just liked the pictures of the fish. The point is that, again, I discovered all sorts of worlds in those books; worlds I had never even dreamt of.

I am fascinated about circuses and sideshows, reading about P. T. Barnum helped inspire that. Reading about Lon Chaney spurred my love of movies, especially classic horror movies. I read a book on Houdini. It's part of why I fell in love with magic.

In my job as a magician, I quickly learned that a good story can make a trick into something more meaningful. In the last few years, I've created "performance lectures" for adults and teens. I've been able to perform them in over 100 libraries, retirement facilities, schools, and social clubs a year. I get to conjure up ghosts, tell the true-life stories of Houdini, Barnum, and Edgar Allan Poe, and share the history of magic as a performing art.

All that time I looked for a way to share my love of Chicago history as well. This book, an expansion of my Chicago Fire lecture, is a result of that search. While I still perform the other programs, *The Essential Great Chicago Fire* has allowed me to step away from the magic and just engage in pure storytelling.

And what better story to tell? No Chicago event has been so important or so mythologized—a cleansing destruction as the prelude to greatness. Almost every major American city faced fire; New York, 1835; Charleston, 1838; Pittsburgh, 1845; Philadelphia, 1865; Portland, 1866; Boston, 1872. Yet, no fire caught the nation's imagination like the fire in Chicago did.

The fire burned for over 31 hours. It destroyed the heart of the city, a path four miles long and nearly a mile wide. Yet, no city ever recovered from a disaster as speedily or spectacularly as did Chicago.

Newspapers said it could only be compared with the London Fire of 1666 and the burning of Moscow in 1812 by Napoleon. But the area destroyed, the boosters boasted, was twice as great as the total area destroyed by both of the earlier fires. Chicago, they believed, had to be first in everything.

No other city commemorates its conflagration on its flag or has one of its most famous landmarks, a structure revered because it survived the flames. For those who lived through it there would always be two Chicagos, the one before the fire and the one after.

Lastly, please remember as you read this, of all the unjust myths concerning the fire, Mrs. O'Leary's cow didn't do it.

Part One
Chicago

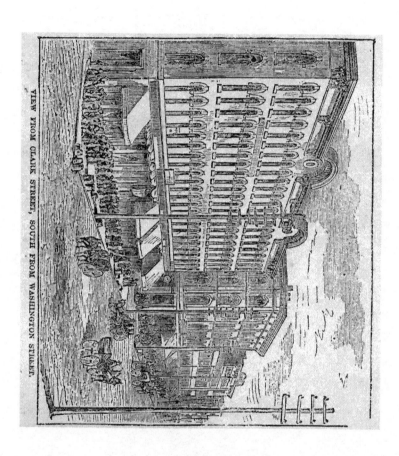

VIEW FROM CLARK STREET, SOUTH FROM WASHINGTON STREET.

6

"All around, on every side in every direction, the vast machinery of Commonwealth clashed and thundered from dawn to dark and from dark till dawn. Here, of all her cities, throbbed the true life—the true power and spirit of America."

-Novelist Frank Norris

I n the years leading up to 1871, Chicago was a boomtown. It grew faster than any other city in the history of the world and was the fourth largest city in America. Between its official date of incorporation in 1837 and 1870, a flood of new settlers swelled the population from 5,000 to over 300,000 people, living in an area six miles long and three miles wide.

Chicago was the "Gem of the Prairie," and the "Queen City of the West." Novelist Henry B. Fuller best captured its character when he wrote, it was "the only great city in the world to which all of its citizens have come for the one common, avowed object of making money."

Chicago embodied the American dream and drew large populations of German, Irish, and Scandinavian immigrants to the city. The immigrants fueled a city of industry, energy, and motion—constant motion.

No American city seemed a better symbol of national industry and progress. It defied nature and built itself on a swamp. A land so forbidding, the Miami Indians refused to settle on it. Wagons carrying supplies to town became stuck in axel deep mud. For a distance of ten miles around town, water on the prairie was up to three feet deep, the coarse prairie grass refusing to let it drain.

In town, it was no better. Shopkeepers amused themselves by

7

posting signs in the mud-clogged streets: "No bottom here," "On his way to the lower regions," and "Shortest road to China." Finally, in 1855, faced with constant flooding and disease, the city lifted itself up and out, raising the streets, sidewalks, and buildings. When the sewage from the new drainage system threatened to pollute Lake Michigan, they reversed the flow of the river away from the lake, saving their drinking water. These acts were representative of the "Chicago Way," bold, daring solutions to problems.

The city positioned itself as the gateway to the developing West. Opening in 1848, the Illinois and Michigan Canal connected Lake Michigan to the Mississippi River and launched Chicago as the largest pork, lumber, and grain market in the country. By 1870, more vessels docked at Chicago than at the ports of New York, Philadelphia, Baltimore, San Francisco, Charleston, and Mobile combined.

The same year the canal opened, however, Chicago gambled its future to a rival means of transportation. In 1847, the city did not have a single mile of railroad track. Ten years later, it was the rail center of the country. Almost all railroads led to Chicago, 100 passenger trains either entered or left the city every day. If you were traveling from the East, you couldn't get anywhere west without stopping in Chicago first.

Even more freight trains passed through the city every day, full of wheat, cattle, and lumber. More than 16 million bushels of wheat were stored in giant grain elevators along the river. There were 21 meatpacking houses around the near south-side Union stockyards. Chicago was an important place for the buying, storing, selling and shipping of goods.

An important place, but still a frontier town, Chicago was always filled with people passing through: tourists, farmers, immigrants, and businessmen—and hustlers who were there to prey on them. A wide-open town, it was a paradise for gamblers, pickpockets, confidence men, and prostitutes.

The "Lager Beer Riots" of 1855 protesting Mayor Levi Boone, who tried to close the saloons on Sundays, assured that Chicago would have no problems with the free flow of alcohol until the 1920s.

Gunfights were so common on Randolph Street that it was known as "Hairtrigger Block" for decades.

The only effort made to change the city's image came from one of its boldest speculators, Potter Palmer. He realized that Chicago would need to have a world-class downtown and set about creating one, starting with a new commercial district.

His plan was to move the main commercial strip from Lake Street to State Street. Lake Street was dirty, cramped, poorly lit, and filled with vagrants. He understood to thrive there was a need to attract female shoppers in great numbers. State Street would be safe, have well lit, wide sidewalks, and be lined with magnificent show windows.

To set the tone, Palmer built a six-story marble-faced emporium at the corner of State and Washington. He talked Marshall Field and Levi Leiter into renting it for the unheard sum of $50,000 a year. They created the most luxurious, opulent store of its kind. The line of carriages stretched for blocks the day it opened.

In the summer of 1870, Potter Palmer announced his engagement to Bertha Honoré. As a wedding gift, Palmer would build his bride the grandest hotel in Chicago. At eight stories, it was the tallest building in the city, and with 225 rooms, the largest hotel in the country. Palmer also billed it as the only fireproof hotel in America. It had telegraphic alarms in each room, hoses on every floor, and a large water tank on the roof. It looked like a fortress and was said to be impregnable.

To the awe of their out of town guests, Chicagoans proudly showed off the grand buildings that made up the rich and beautiful business district. Tall buildings made of study brick, stone and Athens marble.

But Chicago was mostly a false front and the river that created the city also divided it.

There were three main divisions:

The South Division contained the main business district, the most expensive buildings, at $340,000,000 half the assessed value of Chicago. It also contained the worst slums and vice districts in the city. The worst of which being "Conley Patch," run by an aging alcoholic named Mother Conley. The crime and vice riddled Patch was once colorfully called a collection of hundreds of the "dirtiest, vilest, most rickety, one-sided, leaning forward, propped up, tumbled-down, sinking fast, low-roofed, and most miserable shanties."

The North Division was home to the city's finest residential district where Chicago's founders, the "native borns," the urban elite, and captains of industry built their homes and mansions.

Across the "T" of the river was the West Division. Industrial areas dotted the riverbank with working class neighborhoods; immigrant housing, only one-step above the slums, which provided the cheap labor needed to keep the city running.

10

There were more than just the obvious imperfections. Yes, the city had grown quickly, but perhaps too quickly. Buildings were slapped together for maximum profit with little or no regard for construction methods. The *Chicago Tribune* described them as "firetraps pleasing to the eye, nothing more than shams and shingles built by swindling contractors."

The city was almost entirely made of wood.

Durable building materials, such as stone and marble were a mark of opulence rather than customary use. The Chicagoans who pointed out the Athens marble failed to note that it was really limestone with Athens Illinois as the source. The sturdy brick buildings were sometimes only a façade, one brick thick, over a wood frame. Even the buildings of more substantial stuff, and advertised to be fireproof, almost without exception had wooden floors, windows, and doorframes.

Even the cornices on the finest marble buildings were made of inexpensive wood and decorated to look like stone. They had long wooden signs, mansard top stories of wood, wooden roofs covered with felt, tar, or shingles. The fine edifices were interspersed with more simple wooden houses, shops, stables, and saloons.

The slums and the working class neighborhoods were enormous frame warrens, with wooden houses, barns, shacks, tenements, stores, warehouses, and small factories.

Only seventy of the nearly 600 miles of streets within the city limits were surfaced. Fifteen miles were covered with cobblestones or gravel. The other fifty-five were faced with pine blocks, set in the roadway like paving bricks. Another 600 miles of raised wooden sidewalks, some as high as five feet, bound the city in a highly combustible knot.

Not only the construction, but also the contents of the buildings would add fuel to the fire. Inside the stores and warehouses were aisle after aisle of wooden shelves and cases, often containing a myriad of flammable goods.

Long lines of wooden rail cars sat in the rail yards. The grease and oil slicked river was traversed by a dozen wooden bridges and heavily traveled by wooden ships.

Industry lined the riverbanks. Chicago had become a thriving center of woodworking industries. The wood, paint, varnish, even their waste: sawdust and wood shavings were all highly combustible. The seventeen, five story tall grain elevators were tall wooden chimneys full of explosive grain.

Every house and business had its own winter supply of kerosene for lamps, coal and kindling to heat, cook, and run their boilers.

Historian Robert Cromie observed, "It might be said, with considerable justice, that Chicago specialized in the production, handling, and storage of combustible goods."

Part Two
Before the Fire

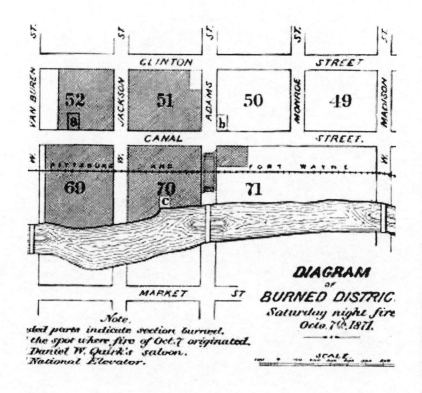

DIAGRAM
OF
BURNED DISTRIC.
Saturday night fire
Octo. 7th 1871.

Note.
ded parts indicate section burned.
the spot where fire of Oct.7 originated.
Daniel W. Quirk's saloon.
National Elevator.

14

"Chicago was then built as if to invite
its destruction in this manner."
-Historian Alfred T. Andreas

I
n 1870 alone, there were 600 reported fires. The fire
department repeatedly requested that a building inspection
department be established and that metal roofs be required for
hotels and other large public buildings. The department asked
the city to install more fire hydrants, build larger water mains, hire
more firemen, and purchase two fireboats with powerful pumps to
protect the river. The city government rejected every one of these
recommendations, insisting that higher taxes and stricter building
codes would have an adverse effect on business expansion.

Of course, ignoring the fact that a business burned to the
ground would also have an adverse effect on business.

Despite ignoring their pleas, the Chicago Fire Department
was bigger and more modern than most, but it was also spread
too thin. Chicago's eighteen square miles was guarded by 185
firefighters with an additional twenty-three men at the
headquarters. All were on call twenty-four hours a day.

Over a period of ten years, the city replaced all the hand-
pumped engines with new horse drawn, steam-driven engines
capable of pouring 600 to 900 gallons a minute on a fire. In
addition, there were twenty-three hose carts, four hook-and-ladder
wagons, and two hose elevators, which could raise the hose to a
height of two stories.

In the summer of 1871, the city had just finished installing a
new network of fire-alarm boxes. The telegraphic network of 172
boxes was supposed to be simple and easy to operate. The alarm

boxes were sturdy iron and contained a simple lever, which could be triggered with one thumb. Instantly transmitted to the courthouse, the signals were then relayed to the fire stations, and tolled out on the giant courthouse bell. To prevent people from turning in false alarms the boxes were locked, the keys entrusted to responsible citizens in nearby residences or businesses.

Augmenting the department was the Insurance Patrol. Financed by merchants and insurance companies, the patrol prowled the business districts with chemical extinguishers mounted on a wagon, putting out small fires.

Chicago's first line of defense was its system of water mains and hydrants. The new fortress-like Water Works, pumping station and water tower, drew water from Lake Michigan through a two-mile tunnel under the lakebed. The water in the tower would be gravity fed to the water mains throughout the city. If need be, the whole of Lake Michigan could be pumped into the city.

Water was in otherwise short supply by October of 1871. It had been a hot dry summer, the second year of a bad drought. No one could remember any worse. Less than five inches of rain had fallen since Independence Day and barely a tenth in the three weeks prior to the fire.

Wells and cisterns dried out. Strong hot prairie winds sucked the moisture from the wood and turned it to tinder. The trees shed their leaves early and lawns went brown like straw. Chicagoans watched as their tar roofs bubbled in the noonday sun.

Chicago was a desiccated husk of a city.

On October 1, there were four alarms and five the next day. On October 3, a half dozen more fires ignited and were put down. The entire first week of October had been a bad one for fires.

The bell rang from the courthouse for each of the twenty-eight significant fires that erupted in the first seven days of the month. The firemen and equipment were becoming worn out. The steamers needed overhaul. Hose was in short supply, much of it old and unfit for use.

At 11 PM, on Saturday, October 7 a fire broke out at the Lull and Holmes Planing Mill, a small woodworking factory located on Canal Street near Van Buren. Adjacent to the mill were two lumberyards, a few houses, more than a few saloons, and a box factory.

The first alarm drew fire equipment from only the immediate area, but the fire, aided by a brisk wind, looked dangerous. A second alarm brought engines from further away. The fire eagerly spread. A third alarm was triggered bringing all available men and equipment to the scene.

Firefighting strategy was simple: Gather whatever engines were available, surround the fire, and pour all the water possible on the entire area whether it was burning yet or not.

By 3:30 AM, the fire was under control, however it would take another twelve hours to completely extinguish it. Twenty buildings were destroyed in a four block square area bordered by Van Buren, Clinton, Adams, and the south branch of the river.

The greater toll was on the fire department. The men were exhausted to the point of collapse. The era's technology forced the men to fight close to the fire. Some had suffered burns, and could barely see through eyes that were red and swollen from the smoke and cinders.

The fact that Chicago had not already burned down was more a matter of luck than manpower or technology. Every time the fire department was able to arrive quickly and managed to contain the fire with their primitive equipment. Early and accurate warning was responsible for a remarkable record of success in fighting fires. Chicago waited for what fire officials insisted could never happen—a fire spotted too late to prevent it from turning into a holocaust.

That morning, while the mill fire still smoldered, the editor of the *Chicago Tribune*, Horace White examined large cinders from the fire that settled around his house more than two miles away. Later, in the *Tribune,* he would write, "For days past, alarm has followed alarm, but the comparatively trifling losses have familiarized us to the pealing of the Courthouse bell, and we have forgotten that the absence of rain for three weeks has left everything in so dry and inflammable condition that a spark might start a fire which would sweep from end to end of the city."

Only a few hours later, the *Tribune's* warning would become a devastating truth.

Part Three
De Koven Street

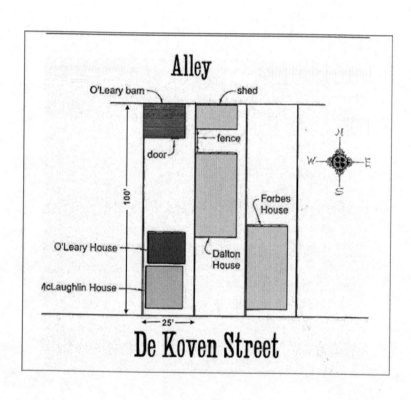

Alley

O'Leary barn

shed

door

fence

100'

O'Leary House

Forbes House

Dalton House

McLaughlin House

25'

De Koven Street

"The feast was spread and only awaited the fiend."
-Historian Robert Cromie

Sunday, October 8 was an unusually warm day for autumn. A brisk prairie breeze blew unabated from the southwest. It did nothing to lessen the heat. The site of the Lull and Holmes fire still smoldered. The excitement over, the thousands of spectators returned to their regular activities.

The property of Patrick and Catherine O'Leary at 137 De Koven Street was typical of the area, narrow and overbuilt. It was twenty-five feet wide and a hundred feet deep. Directly facing the street was a small, shingled house that Mr. O'Leary rented to the McLaughlin family for extra income. Directly behind the main house, the O'Learys lived in a small cottage. At the back of the property, next to the alley, was a barn for Mrs. O'Leary's cows.

Catherine O'Leary kept five cows, a calf, and a horse. She ran a milk route in the neighborhood. The O'Learys were in bed before 8 PM. They had to milk the cows and tend to their deliveries early in the morning.

The fire started about 9 PM.

Daniel "Peg Leg" Sullivan was the first to sound the alarm. There is no way of telling how or why the fire started. The investigation was sloppy, perhaps even willfully so. The testimony by most parties was incomplete, contradictory, and never challenged by the investigators. The final report by the commission determined the fire cause as unknown. (For a full account of the inquiry see: *The Great Chicago Fire and The Myth of Mrs. O'Leary's Cow*, Richard F. Bales.)

What we do know is that it started in the O'Leary barn and it burned quickly. Sullivan managed to get to the barn and release several of the animals, but the fire grew quickly and threatened to overwhelm him. He barely escaped.

The fire spread to a shed attached to the barn. It contained two tons of coal for the winter and a large supply of wood.

The normal neighborhood sounds ended with the screams of FIRE! FIRE! FIRE! People came rushing from their homes with buckets and pots of water. The heat from the fire was so hot that the O'Leary house, forty feet away, began to smolder.

The O'Learys, now awake, defended their property. Repeatedly, they poured water over their home and smothered the flames. In a bit of twisted fate, their home survived the fire with little damage, a fact noticed with some bitterness by their homeless neighbors. (At this writing, the Chicago Fire Academy stands at the site of the O'Leary property, city planners evidently having quite the capacity for irony.)

The dense proximity of the neighboring buildings and the brisk wind created a domino effect. Fire ran along the dry grass and leaves to the fence between the O'Leary and the Dalton's property to the east. The Dalton's shed went up next, then the house. The Daltons had the dubious distinction of being the first family made homeless by the fire.

The fire was fifteen minutes old.

William Lee, a neighbor from across the street, did what no one else had thought to do. He ran three blocks to Bruno Goll's drugstore to sound the fire alarm. What followed was a series of fatal errors that set the fire free.

When Lee reached the drugstore, he demanded the call box key. Bruno Goll refused, insisting that a fire truck had already

22

passed. Lee didn't argue. He hurried back to see his house was about to catch fire. He grabbed his wife, baby, and a few valuables and fled to a vacant lot west of the fire.

From his vantage point, he clearly saw that no fire engine had yet arrived on the scene. In his testimony at the official inquiry into the fire, Bruno Goll claimed that after Lee left the store he triggered not one, but two alarms. Neither signal was ever received at the central alarm office in the Courthouse.

On duty at the Courthouse was Mathias Schafer. His job was to stand watch in the Courthouse cupola a hundred feet above the ground and scan the city for signs of fire. Schafer was showing some visitors around when one of them pointed out the smoke in the distance. Initially, he dismissed it as smoldering from the previous night's fire.

It would be several minutes before he looked back to see flames shooting into the sky. He studied the flames and called down the speaking tube to his assistant to strike the alarm at Box 342 at Canalport and Halsted. It was 9:30 PM. This sent engines racing through the streets—to a location almost a mile away from the O'Leary barn.

Schafer studied the blaze some more and a few minutes later realized his mistake. He ordered Box 319 struck at 12th and Johnson. His assistant, William J. Brown, refused to send a new alarm insisting that it would confuse the situation. The result was that a number of engines and dozens of men were sent on a wild-goose chase and did not get to the fire until it was too late to control. Worse, two powerful engines nearby, capable of throwing 700 and 900 gallons of water a minute on the fire, did not respond even though the O'Leary barn was in their district.

As soon as the fire started people swarmed to De Koven Street, some to help, some to watch. Not so different from modern times, fires were exciting and dramatic entertainment.

One of the first on the scene was a twenty-year-old reporter for the *Chicago Evening Post*, Joseph E. Chamberlin. "I was at the scene in a few minutes," he wrote. "The fire had already advanced a distance of about a single square through the frame buildings that covered the ground thickly north of De Koven Street and east of Jefferson Street—if those miserable alleys shall be dignified by being denominated streets. That neighborhood had always been a *terra incognita* to respectable Chicagoans, and during a residence of three years in the city I had never visited it."

Chamberlin reveals a disdain for the area and its inhabitants shared by a great many people living in the wealthier sections of the city. This bias would go a long way toward fixing the blame for the fire on the poor and slovenly immigrants of De Koven Street. A member of the "dangerous classes," Mrs. O'Leary became an easy target for anti-Irish, anti-poor prejudices.

The gulf between the Haves and the Have-nots, much along racial lines, would only be magnified in how each was treated after the fire.

Finally, two fire companies, *America* and *Little Giant*, found their way to the fire. (Note: each fire brigade, besides being numbered, was given a nickname, *Little Giant* after the diminutive, but powerful U.S. Representative from Illinois, Stephen A. Douglas and *America* after…well, you know.) Hoses were rolled out, attached to the hydrants, and the water turned on. *America* was a hose cart and had limited ability to throw water, while *Little Giant* was the oldest engine in service. The newer, more powerful engines were searching for the fire or still in their stations.

"Streams were thrown into the flame, and evaporated almost as soon as they struck it," Chamberlin wrote.

The gusty winds pushed the fire out in two directions. One arm stretched north up Jefferson, while another arm reached out east. There was no way the two fire companies could contain the blaze on two fronts.

By 10 PM, the entire block was almost destroyed. Seven additional fire companies began to arrive, as did the department's Chief Marshal Robert A. Williams. He immediately positioned the engines to surround the fire and douse it. Just as quickly the firemen were engulfed in a wave of withering heat and flames. "Marshal," the men yelled, "I don't believe we can stand it here!"

"Stand it as long as you can," Williams told them, before hurrying to the foreman of another company, John Dorsey. "Turn in a second alarm!" Williams ordered. "This is going to spread!"

Dorsey ran to Goll's drugstore. He pulled the lever in the box and dashed back to the scene of the fire, not realizing he too had made a mistake. He had neglected to pull down the lever four times, which was the special signal for a second alarm. While Goll's other two alarms were phantoms, this one reached the Courthouse. Schafer and Brown heard the alarm, but ignored it, thinking it was simply telling them about the fire for which they already sent an alarm. They failed to call out more engines.

The fire had been burning for almost an hour, and the wind was picking up speed. The firemen on the scene continued to battle in impossible conditions while waiting for reinforcements. The fierce heat was pushing them back. One firefighter, Charles Anderson, recounted how a passing friend scavenged a wooden

25

door and held it like a shield between him and the fire. Anderson thought he could stand fast, but in less than a minute, the door smoldered and caught fire. Anderson tried to fight, then his clothes began to smoke and his leather hat twisted out of shape on his head.

The overworked equipment began to break down. A steam pump stopped working. Hoses burst. William rushed to reposition the engines, but it was too late.

As one firefighter later put it, "From the beginning of that fatal fire, everything went wrong."

Part Four
The Fire Spreads

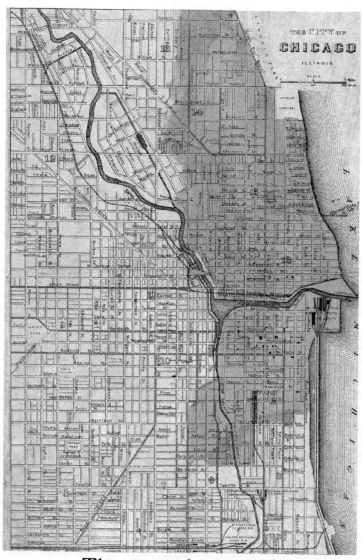

The area destroyed

" This is the last public address that will be delivered within these walls! A terrible calamity is impending over the city of Chicago! More I cannot say; more I dare not utter."

-Lecturer, George Francis Train

Twelve-year-old Claire Innes and her family lived in the South Division, many blocks from the fire. She, like many others, thought there was really no reason to fear. They would see the eerie red glow in the nighttime sky and dismiss it. Most assuredly, the river was an impassible barrier that would protect them.

Tribune editor Horace White summed up the feeling when he wrote, "I had retired to rest, when the great bell struck the alarm, but the fires had been so frequent of late, and had been so speedily extinguished, that I did not deem it worthwhile to get up and look at it, or even count the strokes of the bell to learn where it was."

The fire, though, was already out of control.

The firemen also hoped that once the fire reached a broad street or the river it would run out of fuel and fizzle out, but the intense heat was creating a powerful updraft.

Called convection winds, their formation can cause high-speed winds and fire tornados or fire devils. The super-heated air above the fire rises up because of its lower density and creates an area of low pressure near the flames. This creates a vacuum that sucks in cooler air along the ground. The air getting sucked in is wild and turbulent and begins to rotate around the fire. The process is repeated until a tornado is formed. These spinning, twisting,

29

tornados of fire could rise a hundred feet in the air. They sucked up flaming embers, pieces of cloth, and burning wood and hurled them as far as a half-mile or more. The flaming missiles started new fires far from where they originated, creating new centers of destruction from which fire flowed in all directions.

"The air was filled with sparks and cinders which fell like red rain," one fireman said.

The wind drove the flames along at a brisk pace. Time after time, firemen turned to find tongues of flame licking at their backs as wind-blown cinders ignited fires behind their lines. And time after time, the firemen fell back to establish a new line against the advancing fire.

Around 11 PM, a strong updraft lifted up a two-foot firebrand and tossed it into the steeple of St. Paul's Catholic Church, at Clinton and Mather, four blocks behind the firemen's lines. Marshal Williams sent a hook-and-ladder team to squelch the new flare. In possibly the worst quirk of fate ever, in the lots adjacent to the church were numerous homes, saloons, paint shops, a shingle mill, a box factory, several woodworking shops, and, if that wasn't enough, even a match factory.

With more and more area covered by fire, the heat formed gale force gusts of wind, creating whirlpools as the low wind negotiated its way through the street and between buildings. Many survivors said that the wind and fire seemed to come upon them from everywhere at once.

Great throngs of spectators from Conley Patch rushed over the river to watch the spectacle at St. Paul's. An old Irishwoman asked an observer what was burning. He told her it was the church.

"Oh," she said, "God will put it out."

A few minutes later, the roof caved it.

In less than three hours, twenty city blocks crackled and roared as churches, stores, manufacturing plants, homes, shanties, barns, saloons, outhouses, railroad cars, mills, and fire equipment were consumed by the ravenous fire. The firemen in its path were driven from corner to corner by an implacable tidal wave of flame. Often they escaped only moments before the last exit closed.

Joseph Chamberlin was still in the West Division when, "I caught the words, 'across the river,' uttered doubtingly by a bystander. The words passed from mouth to mouth, and there was universal incredulity, although the suggestion was communicated through the crowd with startling rapidity."

The crowd started to move east to see if the rumor was really true. "I went with the rest," Chamberlin wrote, "[and] stood on the embankment that had been Canal Street, and perceived, through the clouds of smoke, a bright light across the river."

At 11:30 PM, burning debris from St. Paul's was blown across the river to the new, and yet unoccupied, $80,000 Parmelee Omnibus and Stage Company horse stable at Franklin and Jackson.

About thirty minutes later, a burning shingle sailed into the open tar storage tank of Barrett & Arnold, a manufacturer of roofing material. A sheet of fire rushed up and within a minute spread to the adjoining coal shed of the Chicago Gas Light and Coke Company at Franklin and Adams, commonly known as the South Side Gas Works.

The firemen wouldn't get near the Gas Works for fear of explosion. In the face of the ongoing calamity, many errors were made. Considering the onslaught of sparks and heat, it was likely nothing could have saved the Gas Works anyway, but there was little chance of explosion. Before the fire even jumped the river, Superintendent Thomas Ockerly recognized the danger. He wisely transferred the reserve gas out of the division to reservoirs on the North Side preventing a catastrophic explosion.

The destruction of the Gas Works plunged the South Division into darkness; the streets bathed only by the fire's lurid yellow-red glow.

At about 12:30 another flying brand crashed into a three-story tenement nearby. It flared up "like a lucifer match," said one survivor. This was the infamous Conley Patch. A third area of fire established itself in the southern part of the Patch, near the Van Buren Street Bridge.

The fire gluttonously devoured the densely packed, dilapidated shacks and shanties. Many of the men of the Patch were out in the West Division at the time, enjoying the free entertainment of watching someone else's property being destroyed. The women and children were left alone when the flames swooped down upon them. They rushed into the streets clutching what simple possessions they could carry. Many thought it was the end of the world, a cleansing of biblical proportions.

The fire moved swiftly and unpredictably. Most of the Patch escaped, but some—mostly the sick and elderly—were overrun by a moving wall of fire one thousand feet wide and over a hundred feet high.

Fireman Thomas Byrne said, "You couldn't see anything over you but fire. No clouds, no stars, nothing else but fire."

It is in Conley Patch that the "death harvest" began.

Part Five

Chaos

"The dogs of hell were upon the housetops."
-Tribune editor, Horace White

The entire city was now imperiled. In some places, even the grease and oil polluted river caught fire igniting wooden bridges and cargo ships. Thanks to the heroic efforts of the tugboats to tow them to safe waters, only a small percentage of the ships were destroyed.

Horace White finally got out of bed when he heard the courthouse bell tolling a General Alarm. The alarm distinguished a great fire from a small one. When he left his house, he discovered the true magnitude of the fire. It spread so rapidly that it was only five blocks away from his home at Michigan and Adams.

"The dogs of hell were upon the housetops of LaSalle and Wells Streets, just south of Adams," he said, "bounding from one to another. The fire was moving…like an ocean surf on a sand beach. It had already traveled an eighth of a mile and was far beyond control. A column of flame would shoot up from a burning building, catch the force of the wind, and strike the next one, which in turn would perform the same direful office for its neighbor. It was simply indescribable in its terrible grandeur."

Claire Innes woke to a pounding on her bedroom door. Her mother yelled that the fire had crossed the river and was coming towards their home near LaSalle and Jackson. Claire described her experiences in the fire years later.

"I could hear other voices shouting the same thing, so I went to the window. It was very bright, though not as bright as noontime as some have said. There were people everywhere, some going toward the fire for a better view, others away from it. A cart

35

was stationed in front of the house and I could see the family—father, mother and the children—loading furniture, bags, and bundles and the like. I dressed and went downstairs where my family was waiting.

"We all took a bundle and left the house, which Father bolted as he would if we were going on a picnic. There was fire to the west and in places it had gotten behind the house as well, though it was still at a distance. We were to find Clark Street and take that street to the river and a bridge. The river was quite wide there and once we were across we would be safe—or so we were promised."

In some places the sidewalks were jammed, but crowds were reasonably calm. In other places it was chaos—panic stricken, clad in only their nightclothes, many people rushed directionless through the maze of buildings.

The streets were clogged with horse drawn wagons and daring pedestrians moving slowly and fighting for space. The thundering drays and the frantic shouts of the drivers all adding to the confusion and panic.

"Our boys ran at full speed," Mrs. Alfred Hebard, an Iowan traveling through the city described, "and we followed, crossing the State Street Bridge amid a shower of coals. The crowd thickened every moment; women with babies and bundles, men with kegs of beer—all jostling, scolding, crying, or swearing."

Claire's father was upset and repeatedly admonished the children to stay close together and hurry.

"We went two or three blocks, I don't remember exactly how many...when movement became impossible. Sparks and cinders now began to fall all around us and I saw a window awning of a

36

house catch fire…Ahead of us there was much shouting and then the crowd began to push back on us. Father told us to drop our bundles and hold hands, but I did not drop mine. The crowd moved forward a little, then people began turning and pushing against us. There was no resisting the crush and we were swept along. I turned around at some point and saw a building burst into flames as if it were built of dry straw."

The tremendous heat often resulted in buildings combusting spontaneously far in advance of any flame.

Claire felt like a leaf in a great rushing river as the retreat turned into a stampede. The wind swirled, like a storm and was filled with cinders like a scalding snow. She had to shield her eyes to keep from being blinded by the hot ash.

Suddenly, in the crush, a short, tough man grabbed at her bundle. "I would not let it go. I called for father and almost lost my bundle except another man took hold of the first man and dragged him away. When I turned, I could not find Father or Mother or my sisters or brothers. I ran down the sidewalk after them, calling their names and searching everywhere for a familiar face. They were gone—into the smoke and dark and falling fire. I stood near the corner hoping Father or Mother would return for me, and would have stayed there throughout the night except the building up the street began to burn, and then the roof of another and the mob came back at me and I was once again forced to move."

At some point Claire escaped the stream of humanity when she ducked into an alley between two shops. She looked for her family.

"I looked at every face, but I could not find them. When everyone had gone by, I stood in the middle of the sidewalk and shouted for them. It was no use. Except for a few still observing the fire's approach or dragging their possessions to safety, I was alone on the street."

Joseph Chamberlin roamed the streets for hours dodging the shower of stinging sparks. He made his way to the leading edge of the fire, which had reached Franklin and Randolph. The fire seemed to pour down Randolph gobbling up building after building. Suddenly, "the fire was a mountain over our heads. The barrels of oil in Heath's store exploded with a sound of rattling musketry. The great north wall of the Nevada Hotel plunged inward with hardly a sound, so great the din of the surrounding conflagration. The Garden City House burned like a box of matches. Toward the east and northeast, we looked upon a surging ocean of flame."

Much of the fire department was still at work, even though they knew that the fire would not stop until there was nothing left to burn. Engines and men had scattered and were operating on their own. They tried to save anything they could, anything at all. Chief Marshal Williams was hosing down one of the remaining bridge crossings in an effort to keep it open.

Building after building was crashing down in the business district. The brick may have withstood the heat, but the mortar dissolved, the inner wood structures burned, and the walls came tumbling down.

Costing more than twice the original estimate, (not a surprise being Chicago) the million-dollar Courthouse was a center of civic pride and the symbol of the city's prosperity, although, one guidebook called it "the homeliest building in the country." The center of the building was crowned by a two-story tower with a cupola, which contained a four-faced clock, a new five-and-a-half-ton bell, and a fire watchman's platform.

The west wing of the building held the offices of the Mayor, Board of Police and Fire, the fire-alarm telegraph, and other city departments. The east wing housed the Cook County offices, courtrooms, county records, and in the basement, the county jail.

Mathias Schafer had been relieved of his duties by Dennis Deneen at 11 PM, but he stayed around the tower. The grand building, especially the tower, one hundred feet in the air, was exposed to the fiery winds and in constant danger. The two watchmen joined others on the roof to stamp out errant fires. Schafer's clothing even caught fire more than once.

They were fighting against a sucker's odds.

It was only a matter of time before a flaming piece of debris crashed through one of the cupola's windows. It landed in a pile of wood shavings left behind after some construction. Schafer tried, but the mushrooming flames could not be stifled.

He made to escape. Finding the iron stairway down barred by smoke and fire, Schafer was forced to slide down the bannisters, scorching his whiskers and burning his hands and face. It was about 1:35 AM, four and a half hours after the fire started. Schafer and Deneen dashed down to the operations room. They saw flames through the ceiling's cracked plaster. Schafer started the machinery, which would ring the bell automatically as long as it could. The two men then fled to the basement jail to warn of the impending doom.

Within thirty minutes, the bell tower collapsed. The enormous bell, tolling to the last, came crashing down with a roar that was heard a mile away over the bellowing fire.

The basement jail in the east wing was filling with smoke and the prisoners began to scream, afraid of being burned alive. Police Captain Michael Hickey also worried about the prisoners and he took responsibility for them. Those charged with murder were taken away in handcuffs and under guard to the North Side. The rest were released into the streets.

Just south of the fire, former Alderman James Hildreth had gotten hold of 2,500 pounds of explosives and was setting off charges to level buildings. He was trying to rob the fire of fuel and create a firebreak. His first few efforts were dismal failures. He knew little about demolitions. He wasn't the sort of man to give up easily; it might take a few attempts, but he knew he'd get the hang of it.

When Hildreth and his wrecking crew did get the hang of it, they blew up thirty or forty buildings. He toppled every building on the north side of Harrison Street from State Street to Wabash, North on Wabash to Congress, and South on Congress to Michigan. Some historians credit him with helping stop the southward progression of the fire; others credit him with being little more than a menace.

Part Six
Fire Everywhere

CHICAGO FIRE VIEWS—FIELD, LEITER & CO.'S STORE.

Marshall Field Store

*"From that moment the flames ran in our
direction, coming faster than a man could run."*
-Mrs. Aurelia King

Flaming chunks of debris started new fires wherever they fell. As early as 1:30 AM, fire crossed the river to the North Division. A carpentry and paint shop at Lill's brewery, near the lakeshore just south of Chicago Avenue, began burning. Fortunately, it was an isolated spot, the fire barely spread.

An hour later, the burning began in earnest. A rail car full of kerosene on the North Western tracks, Wright's stables just east of the State Street Bridge, and the bridge itself caught fire within minutes of each other. It spread to some of the houses to the northeast.

One by one, building by building, block by block, the fire relentlessly surged forward. The main thrust made a narrow path straight towards the Water Tower.

Tens of thousands of people scrambling for their lives became trapped and confused, most stumbled their way to escape through the blinding smoke and showers of sparks. Those that didn't perished as they became trapped in the labyrinth of streets and alleys.

Scores of people had no other choice but to wade into the cold waters of Lake Michigan. Hundreds would stand for hours, forced into water up over their shoulders by the hot sparks. They turned their backs to the awful spectacle, the air too hot to breathe, and they watched over each other, smothering the cinders igniting their hair and clothing.

After dunking his wife in the water to put out her smoldering hair, one woman asked her husband to drown her rather than let her be burned up.

In the middle of this smoke and fire and panic was twelve-year-old Claire Innes—alone. She didn't know where her family was, but she knew she had to keep moving.

"I ran up the street after the rest. The fire was everywhere, and the crowd split up, everyone taking the route they thought safest. I followed the largest number for a block, but they scattered at every alley and turn until I decided to choose my own direction. Fire and smoke and dust were everywhere, so I ran up the street with the least of it."

Claire had no idea where she was, but continued to run until she could run no more.

"I was all turned around and more tired than I can ever remember being. I was choking on the smoke and dust and I looked for a quiet place to rest. A little along the way I came to a wide alley and went down it to an empty section filled with bricks and boards, barrels, and ladders and such."

No sooner than she sat down at the construction site, a man hurried past. Then a second. A third went by and yelled something to her over his shoulder, but she didn't understand because he spoke German.

When she looked to where the men had just been, she saw smoke and fire blocking the way. It startled her, how quickly the fire had appeared. She went to follow the men, but they were already gone and a curtain of smoke and fire dropped down on that end of the alley also.

Claire was trapped, locked in by the fire. She tried to find

44

escape between the buildings, but she could only get within thirty feet of the thick smoke before being driven back. "The heat was like that of an oven. I tried to open the door to a building, but found it bolted. Smoke was escaping from under the other doors, so I gave up hope of finding any safety through them."

As each of the surrounding buildings succumbed, the rain of burning embers became an unbearable torrent. Claire retreated, seeking the safest, coolest place. She found herself back at the construction site.

"I cannot say I actually decided to hide behind the bricks since I could not hear myself think in the terrible noise. I did not even look at the fire, but hid my face in the dirt and pulled my bundle over my head."

The pile of bricks Claire hid behind protected her from the severest heat and much of the flying debris. She had a great amount of luck on her side as well.

Most of the buildings that boxed her in did not collapse and never released the full wave of killing heat and fire. The walls that did collapse fell far enough from her that she was not crushed.

Time had no meaning in the din that surrounded Claire. She hid her head beneath her bundle and said her prayers for many minutes. It probably took an hour or more for the fire to abate.

Once it lessened, Claire peeked out. The sight astonished her; formerly sturdy brick buildings now blackened skeletons. There was no time to stand and stare, Claire needed to move.

"My legs and arms and back were all burnt where my dress caught fire. I put out the fire and made ready to leave, which was not easy as the openings were blocked with brick and burning wood and smoke. I called out again and again and at last a voice called back to me through the smoke. He told me to stand away from there as a wall of the building might fall on me. This made me even more alarmed, but I did not want to stay in the alley alone, so I began climbing. The bricks were still hot—very hot—but I found that if I did not stop my feet were not burnt so bad."

Claire made it through the smoke and to the street, but no safety was found. All around her buildings were burning and collapsing, the air pierced every so often by explosions of flammable liquids. This only spurred her on to move.

She still had to find her family in all this.

In the mostly affluent residential North Division, another story was unfolding. The prejudiced view of the time was that the "better class" would remain calm and law abiding in the face of an emergency. Alexander Frear, a visiting New York Alderman, witnessed anything but a civilized evacuation.

"All the mansions were being emptied with the greatest disorder and the greatest excitement. Nobody endeavored to stay the flames now. A mob of men and women, all screaming and shouting, ran about wildly, crossing each other's paths, and intercepting each other as if deranged. We tried to force our way along the avenue, which was already littered with costly furniture, some of it burning in the streets under the falling sparks, but it was next to impossible. I saw a woman kneeling in the streets with a crucifix held up before her and the skirt of her dress burning while she prayed. We barely passed before a runaway truck dashed her to the ground. Loads of goods passed us…that were burning on the trucks, and my nephew says that he distinctly saw one man go up to a pile of costly furniture lying in front of an elegant residence and deliberately hold a piece of burning packing board under it until the pile was lit."

The heat was so intense it melted iron and steel, turned stone into powder, and marble and granite to lime. Trees exploded from the boiling of their own sap.

All the senses were inundated by the nightmarish cacophony, well described by an unidentified survivor, "Everywhere dust, smoke, flames, heat, thunder of falling walls, crackle of fire, hissing of water, panting of engines, shouts, braying of trumpets, roar of wind, tumult, confusion, and uproar."

SCENE IN DEARBORN STREET WHEN THE FIRE REACHED THE TREMONT HOUSE.

48

Part Seven
Hope Lost

Unknown Ruins

*"Everyone about me likened the awful scene
to his fancy of the Judgment Day."*
-Tribune Owner Joseph Medill

The flames snaked toward Chicago's last hope, the Water Works. Historian Joseph Kirkland wrote, it moved "like a wild beast intent on destroying its worst enemy, the enemy which it must either kill or be killed by."

Shortly after 3 AM, D.W. Fuller, a city employee, saw a flaming piece of timber about twelve feet long, sailing in on the wind. It narrowly missed the Water Tower and crashed into the pumping station's roof. The timber cracked the protective slate roof. Fingers of fire pried through and began clawing at the wooden underroof. Soon the roof was gripped in a fist of fire.

In less than an hour, the roof collapsed.

The pumps stopped. The only water available was the "dead" water left in the mains and in the Water Tower. When that was exhausted, the streams from the firemen's hoses died. With hydrants now useless, the fire engines were ineffective except along the river and the lakeshore.

Chicago was now utterly helpless.

By 6 AM Monday morning, the fire had raged for nine hours and the flames marched north with little opposition. Chicago's Mayor, Roswell B. Mason, received a steady stream of reports about the spread of the fire and prayed for a miracle. Finally, he gave up hope and sent urgent telegrams to the surrounding cities and towns.

CHICAGO IS IN FLAMES
SEND YOUR WHOLE DEPARTMENT TO HELP US

Aid came from Milwaukee, Cincinnati, Dayton, Louisville, Detroit, Port Huron, Bloomington, Springfield, Janesville, Allegheny, and Pittsburgh. It would take hours and days to arrive. Some cities sent steamers and ladder wagons, others sent badly needed hose and fresh fire fighters. They did this often at great risk to their own cities. Milwaukee put three steamers and their crews on a train, leaving that city with only one working engine.

After narrowly escaping the flames the night before, Joseph Chamberlin went west up Madison Street into an area untouched by fire and was startled when he met groups of shop girls on their way downtown as usual, bearing lunch baskets, as if nothing had happened. They saw the fire and smoke before them, but could not believe that the city, with their means of livelihood, had been swept away during the night.

The last group of buildings to fall on the South Side was Terrace Row, a connected block of elegant stone houses facing the lake on the spot where the Auditorium Building now stands. Just before noon, flames began shooting from the windows of the home of William Bross, co-owner of the *Chicago Tribune*. "Quickly and grandly they wrapped up the whole block and away it floated in black clouds over Lake Michigan."

Before the fire consumed the entire block, the hotelier John B. Drake, on his way back from inspecting the ruins of his Tremont House, walked past the Michigan Avenue Hotel. A sudden hunch made him enter, find the owner, and he offered to buy the hotel.

The owner thought he was crazy; surely, the flames would

52

seize the building at any moment. Drake said he would take the risk and sealed the deal with a down payment of the $1,000 he had in his pocket.

As he walked away, Drake had the uneasy feeling he might have made a foolish bargain. However, two fire engines, the *Brown* and the *Rice* set up a relay line from the lake, one engine feeding the other—they poured water onto the hotel, saving it. John Drake was one of the luckiest men in Chicago that day.

Those in the North were still fighting the swift moving fire. For some there was no escape except to the Sands, about where the Tribune building is today, an area once inhabited by gamblers and prostitutes, now mostly abandoned. Those not trapped on Sands, between the fire and the Lake, escaped to the 230 acre Lincoln Park and the abandoned city cemetery just south of it.

"The cry was North! North!" recalled Mrs. Aurelia King, the wife of a city merchant.

The park was a long finger of wooded land. Thousands of the displaced were there, some huddling for protection in the empty holes left by the recently relocated graves.

There were even more refugees on the prairie, west of the city, almost thirty thousand. The McCormicks and other North Side elites camped on the bare ground next to the "lowliest vagabond and the meanest harlot…all reduced to a common level of misery."

By 11 PM Monday night, the fire had been burning for twenty-seven hours.

Twenty-seven hours of running, panic, destruction, and death.

But at 11 PM that Monday something happened that would later be called a miracle. Mixed with the smoke and falling embers, people felt a sprinkle of cool water on their faces. They began shouting for joy. They hugged each other, cried with each other, and danced with abandon.

As the hours passed, the drizzle turn to a steady rain, doing what no one in Chicago could. It halted the fire. Pockets of fire would burn and smolder for days and weeks afterward, mostly in basement coal piles.

Now a new drama was just beginning.

Part Eight
After the Fire

Madison St. near Market St.

"Where shall I begin? How shall I tell the story that I have been living during these dreadful days?"
-An Unidentified Survivor

Nearly 100,000 people were homeless. Many, like Claire Innes, separated from their families, now had the difficult task of searching for their loved ones. Tuesday morning, the rain woke Claire, who had collapsed from exhaustion. She went searching for something to eat.

She never said where she found food or what she ate, but afterward, she set out to find her house, or what was left of it. Maybe her parents would look for her there. She didn't want to miss them. She knew of no other way to find them.

She wandered through the burned district at mid-morning and was surprised by the activity she found.

"The streets were crowded with wagons, coming and going, while people stood in groups looking at the smoking black heaps that were once houses and stores and churches. At one place, I saw a woman collecting pots and pans and arranging them on a stove, as if she were about to cook a meal. Next, I came upon several men gathered around a charred lump, and each man was shaking his head sadly. I did not want to think about what it might be, so I did not stop."

For many days afterward, bodies would be dug out of the rubble. The corpses—or what was left of them—were laid out in rows on the floor of a makeshift morgue. It was a busy place. The police permitted four or five persons at a time to enter and view the bodies, looking for missing relatives and friends. A pile of pine coffins stood nearby for use when bodies were identified. A great number of sightseeing ghouls also came to inspect the ghastly remains.

No one ever knew how many died. Only 120 bodies would be recovered, though officials estimated 300 people perished in the conflagration. Some of the unaccounted certainly slipped into the river and were washed away.

Alexander Frear spoke of one such soul. "The rail of the bridge was broken away. How many people were pushed over the bridge into the water I cannot tell. I myself saw one man stumble under a load of clothing and disappear…"

Entire families were believed to have been incinerated, their ashes cast to the winds, leaving no trace of a life or a death.

When the first newspapers appeared a day later, the pages were filled with hundreds of personal ads pleading for any communication from family or friends.

After passing the charred corpse, Claire walked one block after another. It was disorientating; all looked the same. The street signs, familiar landmarks, all gone. She had to ask directions several times until she found what she was told was her block.

"Everything was gone. Where our house had been was nothing but a pile of brick and ash and nothing else. I looked all around, but nothing was the same. I had hoped my parents would be waiting for me, but no one was there. There was not much I could do except stay and wait all day."

Most of Chicago was exhausted, stunned by the immensity of the damage. Though not everyone was paralyzed with shock, some found opportunity as best they could. Margaret O'Toole opened a stand selling chestnuts on Lake Street. William Kerfoot opened a real estate office. The crudely painted sign on his shack, currently on display at the Chicago History Museum, read: "All gone but wife, children, and energy." As the debris cooled, enterprising children dug out melted candleholders, blackened plates, fused together pieces of silverware and made a brisk trade selling them to tourists. H.S. Everhart bought the 7,200-pound remains of the Courthouse bell. He melted it down and made souvenir bells and other trinkets.

Claire Innes sat and waited.

"I do not know how long I waited, but it felt like a very long time. Smoke filled the air and made breathing difficult, and sometimes a great cloud of it would conceal everything. People were all around, but I did not recognize anyone and no one recognized me."

She must have gotten restless because she decided to stroll down the block. She hadn't gone very far before she spotted a familiar figure in the distance. "I saw a man pacing nervously—and it was Father! I had been waiting in front of the wrong house all along. You can imagine the reunion that followed."

She learned that her whole family survived and was staying with a generous family who had opened their doors to them.

Thousands were able to find temporary shelter in other parts of Chicago, some abandoned the city, but some sixty-five thousand people were in desperate need. Fifty thousand army tents were pitched to house the poor. News spread so quickly that by late Tuesday morning fifty train cars of provisions had already arrived.

Aid came in from all across the country and from over twenty-five foreign nations. Cincinnati raised $160,000 for relief by sunset Monday as the fire still burned. Milwaukee made up a special train of supplies. The schools there were closed and business suspended as everyone helped with the collection. St. Louis had a relief train in route on Tuesday. In New York City, wagons went up and down Fifth Avenue with signs that read:

GIVE US CLOTHING FOR THE FIRE SUFFERERS!

Tuesday afternoon the first loads of lumber were delivered to the relief society. The building committee gave enough wood to build a single room structure to anyone who applied. They came in two sizes: twelve-by-sixteen feet and sixteen-by-twenty. All that was required was a place to put the shanty and the ability to nail it together.

The *Chicago Evening Post* called it, "a night of horror, never before equaled on the continent."

The *New York Tribune* wrote, "Since yesterday, Chicago has gained another title to prominence. Unequalled before in enterprise and good fortune, she is now unapproachable in calamity."

It was one of the great urban catastrophes of modern times. The Great Fire burned over 2,100 acres, a swath four miles long and nearly a mile wide through the heart of the city. Property worth $190 million, 73 miles of streets and 17,420 buildings were destroyed.

The West Division, where the fire started, suffered the least damage: 500 modest homes and businesses were lost.

In the South Division, site of the business center, a total of 3,650 buildings fell, including 1,600 stores and 60 factories.

The North Division was the hardest hit, of the 13,800 prefire structures in this mostly residential division, only 500 remained intact.

Inside the Courthouse, all the public records establishing title to every piece of real estate in Cook County went up in flames. Fortunately, three small abstract companies managed to rescue their holdings. In April of 1872, the Illinois legislature passed the Burnt Records Act and those documents were made admissible as evidence in court.

Lost were the Post Office, the Chamber of Commerce, major banks, train stations, most churches, all the newspaper offices including the "fireproof" Tribune building, Col. Wood's museum with its 100,000 curiosities, the entire collection of the Chicago Historical Society including an original copy of the Emancipation Proclamation and President Lincoln's walking stick, most theaters, music halls, and hotels—many of those buildings consumed in just minutes.

A little over half of the $88 million worth of claims were paid out as many insurance companies went bankrupt under the weight of the debt.

After the ruins cooled, many of the bank vaults were dug from the debris and opened. Much of their assets were saved.

Marshall Field and his employees carted off $600,000 worth of merchandise from his store, while another $2.5 million burned with the building. Field and his partner, Leiter, found a temporary site for their store in a brick barn on the South Side.

In the early hours of the fire, the architect of the Palmer House, John M. Van Osdel, buried the building blueprints in the basement and covered them with thick layers of sand and clay. After the fire, when he dug up the perfectly preserved plans, he became convinced of a new method of fireproofing buildings with clay tiles.

Not everyone had such good fortune. Isaac Arnold, a founding father of the city, was about to begin working on a biography of Abraham Lincoln. His personal library housed some 10,000 books, including ten thick volumes of letters from Lincoln, Grant, McClellan, Sherman, and Seward. He collected the speeches, writings, and state papers of the martyred President. He owned some of the most valuable paintings in Chicago. Rather than clear the house of what he could, he and his staff tried to put out the small fires erupting on the property. There were too many and the water supply ran out. In trying to save everything, Arnold was unable to save anything.

A week after the fire, John B. Drake returned to the Michigan Avenue Hotel with the balance due on his new purchase. The seller refused to conclude the deal. Drake walked out, but soon returned with several large men. Placing his watch on the table, he told the man that he had five minutes to complete the agreement or he would be thrown in the lake.

Drake renamed the hotel Tremont House, after the building he lost in the fire—it became a landmark, marking the southern boundary of the fire.

It was business as usual, the "Chicago way."

Part Nine
Hope Regained

State Street 1905

"We have lost money, but we have
saved life, health, vigor, and industry.
Let the watchword henceforth be
Chicago shall rise again!"
-Joseph Medill

E ven before the rebuilding of the city began, William Bross
went to New York to buy new equipment for the *Tribune.*
The first fire survivor to reach the city, he was interviewed
wherever he went. He used each opportunity to be a booster for
the city. "Go to Chicago now!" he coaxed, "Young men, hurry
there! Old men, send your sons! Women, send your husbands!"
Chicago, he predicted, "will be rebuilt in five years, and will have a
population of a million by 1900." (It reached that number by
1890.)

Survivors had awful stories to tell, but the disaster fell heaviest
on the poor. Most of them had no family or friends to get help
from. They had to stand in food lines and spend their nights
searching for safe, dry places to sleep and fought off the starving
rats and dogs, which invaded their camps. When they applied for
help through the Relief and Aid Society, they were investigated to
see if they were not pretending to "want."

The wealthy received special attention from the Society,
getting aid directly without having to go to distribution centers,
where they would have to line up with the unwashed. The Society
explained that these people "were not accustomed to exposures
and hardships, which were easily borne by the laboring people."
Most of the well-off didn't need the aid anyway. They were able to
rely on maids, valets, and drivers in domestic service, temporary

paid labor, and the helping hands of friends. These men and women drew upon a wide range of resources to protect and sustain themselves and their families.

One month after the fire, Fredrick Law Olmstead's "Chicago in Distress" appeared in *The Nation* and captured the mood of the city as it faced the immense task of rebuilding. "For a time men were unreasonably cheerful and hopeful. Now, this stage appears to have passed. In the place there is sternness; but so narrow is the division between this and another mood, that in the midst of a sentence a change of quality in the voice occurs, and you see that the eyes have moistened." Chicago's immediate rush of hope had given way to a fight for survival in the face of the enormous task of rebuilding.

Water became a precious commodity. Refugees swarmed the water carts that moved through the city streets. Workers toiled around the clock to repair the engines of the Water Works. They also needed an alternate source of power. A large locomotive engine was rigged to the pumps and set to work, nearly a third of the city had water. By the beginning of November, the first boiler was brought online and water pulsed through most of the giant arteries of the city.

However, no one considered the hazards that might result from the stagnant water in the pipes. A wave of typhoid spread over the city lasting over two weeks. Children were especially hard hit.

At the same time, a building frenzy had begun. Wages also rose along with the need for workers. Unskilled laborers commanded two dollars a day, while skilled carpenters and bricklayers got between five and ten dollars. (About $100 to

$200 dollars a day in 2013 dollars.)

Alfred Sewell, a reporter for the *Chicago Times,* wrote, "builders were busily engaged in constructing scores of one-story sheds for the temporary accommodation of merchants, and what was a fortnight ago one of the finest residence avenues in the world is now lined with board shanties."

Laborers scavenged the debris for undamaged brick and hauled away everything else. Thousands of tons of refuse was carted to the lake and dumped; not only was Chicago swept clean of the fire, but a new lakefront was created.

By the end of 1871, workmen finished or nearly finished 6,000 wooden shanties, 2,000 solid wood-frame buildings, and 500 structures of brick and stone.

Overwhelmed, Alfred T. Andreas wrote, "It [was] common to see ten or a dozen or fifty houses rising at once; but when one looks upon, not a dozen or fifty, but upon *ten thousand* houses rising and ten times that number of busy workmen coming and going, and listens to the noise of countless saws and hammers and chisels and axes and planes, he is bewildered."

By March of 1872, despite an unusually harsh winter, Chicago had nearly twenty miles of stone and brick buildings and tens of thousands of lesser structures completed.

The first phase of Chicago's reconstruction lasted two years and resulted in the rebuilding of the burned out area and the recharging of the economy. Money flowed into the city. Trains still ran to the city. The stockyards and meat packing plants were untouched. In 1872, the Union Stockyards handled twice as many hogs as it did in 1870.

Ironically, most of the structures immediately erected after the

67

fire were little better than the ones that burned down. In the rush to build, construction often started before the architectural plans were completed. As a result, architects relied on old and dangerous habits. By 1874, the rebuilt core of the city looked much the same as the downtown of 1871, just larger and a few stories taller. Which is why in July of 1874, the Little Chicago Fire destroyed eighteen blocks and millions of dollars worth of buildings on the southern edge of the business district. Only after this second fire did the city finally enact stricter building regulations.

By 1880, however, a new generation of architects were about to begin reshaping the urban landscape. Using new technological revolutions in construction, they created the world's first vertical city. Visionary architects like William Jenny, Louis Sullivan, H.H. Richardson, Daniel Burnham and John Root renewed Chicago, building and rebuilding, year after year, a little larger, a few stories taller, and again, a little larger, and a few stories taller.

THE END

Part Ten
Songs and Poems

October 9, 1871:
The Burning of Chicago

Poems of the Great Chicago Fire
Collected and Arranged by
Francis J. Gerty

Chicago
The Hendricks School Press
Mcmxv

Like many catastrophic events, the Great Chicago Fire inspired the imagination of writers of all types. Poets of note, including John Greenleaf Whittier, Bret Harte, and Julia Moore as well as songwriters like George F. Root, were among the many who set the Fire to rhythm, rhyme, and melody. Most, charitably, are poor writing, but I include them for historical purposes.

Poems

"Chicago," by John Greenleaf Whittier

Men said at vespers: "All is well!"
In one wild night the city fell;
Fell shrines of prayer and marts of gain
Before the fiery hurricane.

On threescore spires had sunset shone,
Where ghastly sunrise looked on none.
Men clasped each other's hands, and said:
"The City of the West is dead!"

Brave hearts who fought, in slow retreat,
The fiends of fire from street to street,
Turned, powerless, to the blinding glare,
The dumb defiance of despair.

A sudden impulse thrilled each wire
That signaled round that sea of fire;
Swift words of cheer, warm heart-throbs came;
In tears of pity died the flame!

From East, from West, from South and North,
The messages of hope shot forth,
And, underneath the severing wave,
The world, full-handed, reached to save.

Fair seemed the old; but fairer still
The new, the dreary void shall fill
With dearer homes that those o'erthrown,
For love shall lay each corner-stone.

Rise, stricken city! from thee throw
The ashen sackcloth of thy woe;
And build, as to Amphion's strain,
To songs of cheer thy walls again!

How shriveled in thy hot distress
The primal sin of selfishness!
How instant rose, to take thy part,
The angel in the human heart!

Ah! not in vain the flames that tossed
Above thy dreadful holocaust;
The Christ again has preached through thee
The Gospel of Humanity!

The lift once ore thy towers on high,
And fret with spires the western sky,
To tell that God is yet with us,
And love is still miraculous!

"Chicago," by Bret Harte

Blackened and bleeding, helpless, panting, prone
On the charred fragments of her shattered throne
Lies she who stood but yesterday alone.

Queen of the West! by some enchanter taught
To lift the glory of Aladdin's court,
Then lose the spell that all that wonder wrought.

Like her own prairies by some chance seed sown,
Like her own prairies in one brief day grown,
Like her own prairies in one fierce night mown.

She lifts her voice, and in her pleading call
We hear the cry of Macedon to Paul--
The cry for help that makes her kin to all.

But haply with wan finger may she feel
The silver cup hid in the proffered meal--
The gifts her kinship and our loves reveal.

"The Great Chicago Fire," by Mrs. Julia A. Moore

The great Chicago Fire, friends,
    Will never be forgot;
In the history of Chicago
    It will remain a darken spot.
It was a dreadful horrid sight
    To see that City in flames;
But no human aid could save it,
    For all skill was tried in vain.

73

In the year of 1871,
    In October on the 8th,
The people in that City, then
    Was full of life, and great.
Less than four days it lay in ruins,
    That garden City, so great
Lay smoldering in ashes,
    In a sad and pitiful state.

It was a sad, sad scene indeed,
    To see that fire arise,
And hear the crackling of the flames
    As it almost reached the skies,
And sadder still, to hear the moans,
    Of people in the flames
Cry for help, and none could get,
    Ah, die where they remained.

To see the people run for life;
    Up and down the blazing streets,
To find then, their escape cut off
    By the fiery flaming sheets,
And others hunting for some friend
    That perhaps they never found,
Such weeping, wailing, never was known,
    For a thousand miles around.

Some people were very wealthy
    On the morning of the 10th.
But at the close of the evening,
    Was poor, but felt content,
Glad to escape from harm with life
    With friends they loved so well,

Some will try to gain more wisdom,
    By the sad sight they beheld.

Five thousand people were homeless,
    Sad wanderers in the streets,
With no shelter to cover them,
    And no food had they to eat.
They wandered down by the lake side,
    Lay down on the cold damp ground,
So tired and weary and homeless,
    So the rich, the poor, was found.

Mothers with their dear little infants,
    Some clinging to the breast.
People of every description
    All laid down there to rest,
With the sky as their covering,
    Ah, pillows they had none.
Sad, oh sad, it must have been,
    For those poor homeless ones.

Neighboring Cities sent comfort,
    To the poor lone helpless ones,
And God will not forget them
    In all the years to come.
Now the City of Chicago
    Is built up anew once more,
And may it never be visited
    With such a great fire no more.

"Call for Help for Chicago," by N.S. Emerson

For years our beautiful city
Has grown in her strength and pride,
Strong as an Indian warrior,
Fair as a hunter's bride;
But up from her hearts quick throbbing,
List to our pitiful cry.
"A Demon has been among us,
Help! or we surely die.

"A Demon whose power was stronger
Than the strength of our puny hands,
Who paused not to ask for favors,
But took the wealth from our lands:
We fought him with desperate courage,
He laughed at our fruitless pain,
We begged him to spare our treasures
Alas! that we begged in vain.

"Spare us McVicker's temple,
Home of dramatic art."
The demon shrieked and McVicker's
Was booked for its closing part.
"Spare us our *Tribune* building,
Stately and high and strong,
"Whence the Messenger birds fly daily
To battle against the wrong."

The demon crept over the pavement
And clutched at the pillars fair,
And only a heap of embers
And a wreath of smoke were there.

"Spare us then Collyer's pulpit,
He has fought in the Lords good fight,"
    "And every word he utters
Is an anvil stroke for the right."

    "I am no respecter of person,"
Quoth the demon grim and dread,
    "And Collyer can preach next Sunday
With God's blue sky o'er head."
Thus hath the red browed Fire Fiend
    Stolen our treasures dear,
Sucked out our hearts best life blood,
    And left us to famish here.

Gone are our shrines and altars,
    Gone are the hopes we cherished,
All in one hot breath wasted,
    All in a moment perished,
Lost is the grain we garnered,
    Harvest of years gone by.
Help us, for we are starving,
    Help! or we surely die.

"Chicago," by W.H. McElroy

We used to chaff you in other days,
        Chicago,
You had such self-asserting ways,
        Chicago.
By Jove, but you cut it rather fat,
With your boastful talk of this and that,

77

As if America's hub was at
      Chicago.

We Bohemian boys on the Eastern press,
      Chicago,
We lied about you, and nothing less;
      Chicago.
'T was a way we had--without remorse
To manufacture "another divorce,"
And locate it at--as a matter of course--
      Chicago.

The star of empire on its way West,
      Chicago,
You said, concluded that it was best,
      Chicago,
To fix itself in your special sky,
Unmoved by further claim or cry,
And you hailed the star as "good for high,"
      Chicago.

You called New York--so said, at least,
      Chicago,
Called it *"Chicago of the East."*
      Chicago.
Now, wasn't it cutting it rather fat,
To venture on such a speech as that,
As if the hub was certainly at
      Chicago.

But we loved you in spite of your many airs,
      Chicago,
If it wasn't for wheat there wouldn't be tares,

Chicago,
And so as we heard your trumpets blow,
Loud as theirs were at Jericho,
We said--"Well one thing, she isn't *slow*,"
    Chicago.

And when of your terrible trouble we learned,
    Chicago,
How your fair young beauty to ashes was turned,
    Chicago,
The whole land rose in its love and might,
And swore it would see you through your plight,
And--"Draw by the million on us at sight,
    Chicago."

We used to remark, of course with pity,
    Chicago,
That you were our champion wickedest city,
    Chicago,
And yet, just now, you very well may
Insist with reason we can't gainsay,
That you are *the* power for good to-day,
    Chicago.

For if unto Charity it is given,
    Chicago,
To hide no end of sins from Heaven,
    Chicago,
The Recording Angel his pen may take,
And blot out the record we daily make,
And write on the margin *"for charity's sake,"*
    At Chicago.

Songs

"From the Ruins Our City Shall Rise," by George F. Root

1. Ruins! Ruins! far and wide,
   From the river and lake, to the prairie side,
   Dreary, dreary and darkness falls,
   While the autumn winds moan
      thro' the blackened walls.

Chorus *a tempo*

   But see! the bright rift in the cloud.
   And hear! the great voice from the shore.
   Our city shall rise! yes she shall rise,
   Queen of the west once more.

2. Ruins! Ruins! street and square
   In a hopeless confusion are mingled there,
   Strangely, strangely our old haunts fade
   In the cast open waste that the fire has made.

3. Ruins! Ruins! naught is here
   But the wreck of our homes, and our
      hopes most dear,
   Fallen, fallen in ashes gray
   Where they lie with our wealth and
      our pride to-day.

"Pity the Homeless, or Burnt Out," by James R. Murray

1. Pity the homeless, pity the poor,
   By the fierce Fire fiend forced to your door;
   List to their pleading, list to their cry,
   Pass them not heedlessly by,
   Roused from their slumbers, peaceful and sweet,
   Hastening in terror into the street,
   Leaving behind them treasure most dear,
   Flying in anguish and fear...

chorus:

   Pity the homeless, pity the poor,
   By the fierce Fire fiend forced to your door;
   List to their pleading, list to their cry,
   Pass them not heedlessly by.

2. See how the Fire king leaps in his joy!
   As his dead minions haste to destroy;
   See how the homes, once peaceful and fair,
   Wrapped in the flames, melt in air.
   Haste then, and help them, who from their home
   Shelterless, foodless, wearily roam.
   Pity their anguish, list to their prayers,
   Lighten their labors and cares.

"Lost and Saved," by George F. Root

1. Fairer than the lily, Sweeter than the rose,
Was our little darling, at that autumn twilight's close;
Sweetly she was sleeping in the angel's care,

When we joined the footsteps thronging
    to the house of prayer.

chorus

Strange were the sounds when
    the service was through,
Fierce the red glare that then burst on our view,
Dreadful the words that rose higher and higher,
Lost in the Fire! Lost in the Fire!

Quick we hasten'd homeward,
    But the flames were there,
And the frighten'd crowd were
    surging here and ev'ry where.
Oh, my precious darling, Who can save her now,
For the roof is burning, and
    the chimneys sway and bow.

chorus 2

Still the strange sounds when
    the service was through.
Still the fierce glare bursting red on our view,
Still the dread words rising higher and higher,
Lost in the Fire! Lost in the Fire!

When, oh sight of rapture! At the open door,
Stood the little bare feet on
    the hard and heated floor,
'Mama, come and take me. They said you were here,'
Then we knew the angels saved her, for none else were near.

chorus 3

What tho' the sounds rush'd the wide city through.
What tho' the glare was still bright in our view,
Chang'd were the words that rose
    higher and higher,
Saved from the Fire! Saved from the Fire!

"Passing Through The Fire," by George F. Root

1. Flames! flames! terrible flames!
    How they rise, how they mount, how they fly.
    The heavens are spread with a fierce lurid glare,
    Red heat is filling the earth with air,
    While, mercy! mercy! We hear the despairing ones cry.

chorus: (Moderato)

    Passing thro' the fire! passing thro' the fire,
    And it is our Father's hand,
    Tho' we may not understand
    Why we're passing thro' the fire,
        passing thro' the fire!

2. Flames! flames! terrible flames!
    How they sweep, how they rush, how they roar.
    See the hideous tongues round the roof,
        tree and spire,
    As swells their wild carnival higher and higher,
    Till falling! crashing! Our glorious
        city's no more.

3. Flames! flames! terrible flames!
    What a fearful destruction they bring.
    What suff'ring and want in their train follow fast,
    As forth on the streets homeless

thousands are cast,
But courage! courage! From the mid'st of the
furnace we sing.

"The Billow of Fire," by P. P. Bliss

1. Hark the alarm, the clang of the bells!
    Signal of danger it rises and swells;
    Flashes like lightning illumine the sky,
    See the red glare as the flames mount on high!

Chorus:

Roll on, roll on, oh billow of fire!
Roll on, roll on, oh billow of fire!
Dash with thy fury waves higher and higher!
Ours is a mansion abiding and sure,
Ours is a kingdom eternal secure.

2. On like a fiend in its towering wrath,
    On, and destruction alone points the path,
    "Mercy, oh Heaven," the sufferers wail,
    Feeble humanity naught can avail.

3. Thousands are homeless and quick to their cry,
    Heaven born charity yields a supply,
    Upward we glance in our terrible grief,
    "Give us this day," brings the promised relief.

4. Treasures have vanished and riches have flown,
    Hopes for the present life blasted and gone,
    Courage, oh, brother, yield not to despair,
    "God is our refuge," His kingdom we'll share.

Part Eleven
Joseph Chamberlin

The reporter Joseph Chamberlin's account of the fire, quoted in my lecture, first appeared in *Chicago and the Great Conflagration*, by Elias Colbert and Everett Chamberlin, published in 1871. It is reprinted here in full with minor corrections for clarity.

ACCOUNTS of the experiences of eyewitnesses are like photographic views in conveying to the reader minute facts, which cannot be reached in a general sketch. Accordingly we give several statements—the most graphic, and at the same time strictly truthful, which we have anywhere seen. The first is that of Mr. J. E. Chamberlin, a young journalist, whose curiosity led him to follow up closely the conflagration of the 7th, as well as the Great Conflagration which followed on the 8th and 9th. He says:

"I was at the scene in a few minutes. The fire had already advanced a distance of about a single square through the frame buildings that covered the ground thickly north of De Koven Street and east of Jefferson Street—if those miserable alleys shall be dignified by being denominated streets. That neighborhood had always been a terra incognita to respectable Chicagoans, and during a residence of three years in the city, I had never visited it. The land was thickly studded with one-story frame dwellings, cow-stables, pig-sties, corn-cribs, sheds innumerable; every wretched building within four feet of its neighbor, and everything of wood—not a brick or a stone in the whole area. The fire was under full headway in this combustible mass before the engines arrived, and what could be done? Streams were thrown into the flame, and evaporated almost as soon as they struck it. A single fire engine in the blazing forests of Wisconsin would have been as effective as were these machines in a forest of shanties thrice as combustible as the pine woods of the North. But still the firemen kept at work

87

fighting the flames—stupidly and listlessly, for they had worked hard all of Saturday night and most of Sunday, and had been enervated by the whisky which is always copiously poured on such occasions. I stepped in among some sheds south of Ewing Street; a fence by my side began to blaze; I beat a hasty retreat, and in five minutes, the place where I had stood was all ablaze. Nothing could stop that conflagration there. It must sweep on until it reached a broad street, and then, everybody said, it would burn itself out.

"Ewing Street was quite a thoroughfare for that region. It is a mere alley, it is true, but is somewhat broader than the surrounding lanes. It has elevated board sidewalks, and is passable for teams in dry weather. On that night, it was crowded with people pouring out of the thickly settled locality between Jefferson Street and the river, and here the first panic began. The wretched female inhabitants were rushing out almost naked, imploring spectators to help them on with their burdens of bed quilts, cane-bottomed chairs, iron kettles, etc. Drays were thundering along in the single procession, which the narrowness of the street allowed, and all was confusion.

"When the fire had passed Ewing Street, I hurried on to Harrison, aware of the fact that the only hope for the staying of the conflagration was in the width of that street, and hoping that some more effective measures than squirting of water would be taken at that point. The same scene of hurry and confusion was repeated at Harrison on a larger scale than at Ewing; and that same scene kept on increasing in terror all night long, as the fire moved northward. The crowd anxiously watched the flames as they approached the street, and the universal remark was: 'If it passes this, nothing can stop it but last night's burned district.' At length the fire reached the street, and broke out almost simultaneously for a distance of two squares. The two fire engines which stood in

88

Harrison Street fled in terror. Brands of fire, driven on by the gale, struck the houses on the north side of the street. Though mostly of brick, they ignited like tinder, and the fire swept northward again.

"Again I passed into Jefferson Street; keeping on the flank of the fire. In a vacant square, filled with refugees from the fire and their rescued effects, I stopped a few minutes to watch the fiery ocean before me. The open lot was covered with people, and a strange sight was presented. The fire had reached a better section, and many people of the better class were among those who had gathered a few of their household goods on that open space. Half a dozen rescued pianos were watched by delicate ladies, while the crowd still surged in every direction. Two boys, themselves intoxicated, reeled about, each bearing a small cask of whisky, out of which he insisted upon treating everybody he met. Soon more casks of whisky appeared, and scores of excited men drank deeply of their contents. The result was, of course, that an equal number of drunken men were soon impeding the flight of the fugitives.

"When I reached Van Buren Street, the southern limit of the Saturday night fire, I paused to see the end of the conflagration. A single engine stood on Van Buren Street, doing what seemed to me good service in preventing the fire from eating its way westward, against the wind, which it was apparently determined to do. Suddenly the horses were attached to the engine, and, as soon as the hose was reeled, it disappeared, whirling northward on Jefferson Street. What did it mean? I caught the words,' Across the river,' uttered doubtingly by a bystander. The words passed from mouth to mouth, and there was universal incredulity, although the suggestion was communicated through the crowd with startling rapidity. There was a general movement northward and out of the smoke, with a view to discover whether it was really possible that the fire had been blown across the river, and had started afresh on the south side. I went with the rest, crossed the burnt ground of the night before, stood on the embankment that had been Canal Street, and perceived, through the clouds of smoke, a bright light across the river. I rushed to the Adams-street viaduct and across the bridge. The Armory, the Gas-works, 'Conley's Patch,' and Wells Street, as far north as Monroe, were all on fire. The wind had increased to a tempest, and hurled great blazing brands over our heads.

"At this point my duty called me to my home in the West Division; but within an hour I was back again to witness the doom of the blazing city, of which I then had a full presentiment. The streets on the west side were as light as broad noon. I looked at my watch and saw that it was just two o'clock. As I ran down Monroe Street, with the burning town before me, I contemplated the ruin that was working, and the tears rose to my eyes. I could have wept at that saddest of sights, but I choked down the tears, and they did not rise again that night.

"When I crossed the river, I made a desperate attempt to reach my office on Madison Street, beyond Clark. I pressed through the crowd on Randolph Street as far as LaSalle, and stood in front of the burning Courthouse. The cupola was in full blaze, and presented a scene of the sublimest as well as most melancholy beauty. Presently the great tower was undermined by the fire below, and fell to the bottom with a dull sound and a heavy shock that shook the earth. Somebody called out, 'Explosion!' and a panic ensued, in which everything and everybody was carried westward. Then I went to Lake Street, and found a torrent of sparks sweeping down that avenue. But I pulled my hat about my eyes, buttoned up my coat-collar, and rushed eastward, determined to reach my office. I turned down Dearborn, and leaped through a maelstrom of scorching sparks. The fiery storm at length drove me into an open store, from which the occupants had fled. I seized a large blanket, which they had left on the floor, wrapped it around my head and body, and sallied forth again. I went as far as Washington Street, but any attempt at further progress would have been madness. I beat a hasty retreat to Lake Street, and came down LaSalle again to the immediate neighborhood of the fire.

"And now the scene of confusion had reached its height. Wagons were rushing through the streets, laden with stocks of goods, books, valuable papers, boxes of money, and everything conceivable; scores of men were dragging trunks frantically along the sidewalks, knocking down women and children; fabulous sums of money were offered truckmen for conveyances. The scene was indescribable.

"But, as large as was the number of people who were flying from the fire, the number of passive spectators was still larger. Their eyes were all diverted from the scurrying mass of people around them to the spectacle of appalling grandeur before them. They stood transfixed, with a mingled feeling of horror and admiration, and while they often exclaimed at the beauty of the scene, they all devoutly prayed that they might never see such another. The noise of the conflagration was terrific. To the roar, which the simple process of combustion always makes, magnified here to so grand an extent, was added the crash of falling buildings and the constant explosions of stores of oil and other like material. The noise of the crowd was nothing compared with this chaos of sound. All these things —the great, dazzling, mounting light, the crash and roar of the conflagration, and the desperate flight of the crowd—combined to make a scene of which no intelligent idea can be conveyed in words.

"When it became too hot in Randolph Street, I retired to the eastern approach of the bridge on that street. A knot of men had gathered there, from whom all signs of excitement had disappeared. It was then almost four o'clock, and whatever excitement we had felt during the night had passed away. Wearied with two nights of exertion, I sat upon the railing and looked down on the most appalling spectacle of the whole night. The Briggs House, the Metropolitan House, Peter Schultler's wagon manufactory, Heath & Mulligan's oil establishment, stored five stories high with exceedingly inflammable material, the Nevada Hotel, and all the surrounding buildings, were in a simultaneous blaze. The flames, propelled by variable gusts of wind, seemed to pour down Randolph Street in a liquid torrent. Then the appearance was changed, and the fire was a mountain over our heads. The barrels of oil in Heath's store exploded with a sound like rattling musketry. The great north wall of the Nevada Hotel plunged inward with hardly a sound, so great was the din of the surrounding conflagration.

The Garden City House burned like a box of matches; the rapidity of its disappearance was remarked by everybody. Toward the east and northeast we looked upon a surging ocean of flame.

"Meanwhile a strange scene was being enacted in the street before us. A torrent of humanity was pouring over the bridge. Madison Street Bridge had long before become impassable, and Randolph was the only outlet for the entire region south of it. Drays, express-wagons, trucks, and conveyances of every conceivable species and size, crowded across in indiscriminate haste. Collisions happened almost every moment, and when one overloaded wagon broke down, there were enough men on hand to drag it and its contents over the bridge by main force. The same long line of men dragging trunks was there, many of them tugging over the ground with loads, which a horse would strain at. Women were there, looking exactly like those I had seen all night, staggering under weights upon their backs.

92

Whole establishments of ill-fame were there, their half-dozen inmates loaded into the bottoms of express-wagons, driven, of course, by their' men.' Now and then a stray schooner, which, for want of a tug, had been unable to escape earlier from the south branch, came up, and the bridge must be opened. Then arose a howl of indignation along the line, which, being near, was audible above the tumult. A brig lay above us in the stream, and the captain was often warned by the crowd that he must make his exit at once, if he wished to save his craft—a suggestion the force of which he doubtless appreciated, as he stood upon the quarter-deck calling frantically to every tug that passed.

"I saw an undertaker rushing over the bridge with his mournful stock. He had taken a dray, but was unable to load all of his goods into the vehicle. So he employed half a dozen boys gave each of them a coffin, took a large one himself, and headed the weird procession. The sight of those coffins, upright, and bobbing along just above the heads of the crowd, without any apparent help from anybody else, was somewhat startling, and the unavoidable suggestion was that they were escaping across the river to be ready for use when the debris of the conflagration should be cleared away. But just as men in tine midst of a devastating plague carouse over each new corpse, and drink to the next who dies, so we laughed quite merrily at the ominous spectacle.

"At last it became too warm to be comfortable on the east side of the river. The fire was burning along Market Street, and many were the conjectures whether Lind's block would go. The buildings opposite burned with a furnace-heat, but Lind's block stands now, a monument to its own isolation.

"And then the question was every-where asked, 'Will Chicago ever recover from this blow?' Many suggestions were offered on this subject. The general opinion was that the city could never again obtain a foothold. Said one old gentleman, 'Our capital is wiped out of existence. You never can get what money is stored up out of those vaults. There isn't one that can stand this furnace-heat. Whatever the fire consumes tonight is utterly consumed. All loss is total; for there will not be an insurance company left to-morrow. The trade of the city must go to St. Louis, to Cincinnati, and to New York, and we never can get hold of it again. We couldn't transact any business even if we had customers, for we haven't got anywhere to transact it. Yes, sir, this town is gone up, and we may as well get out of it at once.' Thus all seemed to talk, and there was none of that earnest, hopeful language of which I have heard so much since, and have been rejoiced to hear. But what else could I expect? Those men stood facing the burning city. They saw those great hotels and warehouses toppling, one after another, to the ground. Their spirits were elastic, as subsequent events have proved, but on that terrible night, they wore drawn to their utmost tension, and the cord came near breaking.

"Tired with my two nights' work and of the sad sight before me, I joined the crowd, crossed the river, went up Canal Street and lay down on a pile of lumber in Avery's yard. My position was at the confluence of the north and south branches, directly opposite the middle of the main river, and exactly on the dock. All solicitude for the remaining portion of the city, and all appreciation of the magnitude of the tragedy that was being acted across the river, had left me. I did not care whether the city stood or burned. I was dead, so far as my sensibilities were concerned. Half a dozen fellows—strangers—were with me on the lumber-pile, and were as listless as myself. The chief matter, which seemed to interest them, was the probable weight of one of their party—a fat fellow, whom they called Fred. I became quite interested in the subject, and joined in the guessing. Fred kept us bursting in ignorance awhile, and then, in a burst of confidence, told us he weighed 206, and begged us not to mention it. Meanwhile, Wells Street Bridge

94

took fire, and, as affording something novel, attracted our attention for a few minutes. The south end of the bridge caught alight, and then the north end. But the north end burned less rapidly than the south, and soon outbalanced the latter, when, of course, the whole structure tipped to the northward, and stood fixed, one end in the water, at an angle of about sixty degrees. Then the fire communicated with the whole framework, till the bridge looked like a skeleton with ribs of fire. But presently the support underneath burned away; then the skeleton turned a complete summersault and plunged into the river, as if, warmed into life, it had sought refuge from the flames which were consuming it."

[Our contributor here details his adventures upon the north side, which were not of particular moment.]

"When I had regained a footing in the favored West Division, it was seven o'clock. Then a curious-looking crimson ball came up out of the lake, which they said was the sun; but oh how sickly and insignificant it looked! I had watched that greatest of the world's conflagrations from its beginning to almost its end; and although the fire was still blazing all over the city with undiminished luster, I could not look at it. I was almost unable to walk with exhaustion and the effects of a long season of excitement, and sought my home for an hour's sleep. As I passed up West Madison Street, I met scores of working girls on their way ' down town,' as usual, bearing their lunch-baskets as if nothing had happened. They saw the fire and smoke before them, but could not believe that the city, with their means of livelihood, had been swept away during that night."

THE
GREAT FIRE OF CHICAGO!

BEING

A CONCISE ACCOUNT

OF THE

ORIGIN, PROGRESS, AND CONCLUSION OF THIS TERRIBLE FIRE,

The Greatest the Civilized World has ever Known,

BURNING A DISTRICT OF 60 MILES OF BUILDINGS, OR
100 MILES IF PLACED SIDE BY SIDE.

THRILLING ACCOUNTS!
WONDERFUL ESCAPES!!
INTERESTING ANECDOTES!!!

A COMPILATION OF FACTS FOR PRESERVATION.
EDITED BY GEORGE L. BARCLAY.

SCENES AS DESCRIBED BY EYE-WITNESSES.

PHILADELPHIA, PA.
PUBLISHED BY BARCLAY & CO.,
No. 21 North Seventh Street.

Part Twelve
Isaac Arnold

CHICAGO

AND THE

GREAT CONFLAGRATION.

BY

ELIAS COLBERT

AND

EVERETT CHAMBERLIN.

WITH

NUMEROUS ILLUSTRATIONS, BY CHAPIN & GULICK,

FROM

Photographic Views taken on the Spot.

CINCINNATI AND NEW YORK: C. F. VENT.
CHICAGO: J. S GOODMAN & CO. | PHILADELPHIA: HUBBARD BROS.
BOSTON: EDWARD F. HOVEY. AUBURN, N. Y.: F. M. SMITH.
SAN FRANCISCO: F. DEWING & CO.
1871.

Here also is the full account of Isaac N. Arnold's harrowing experience in the fire as it appeared in *Chicago and the Great Conflagration*, by Elias Colbert and Everett Chamberlin, published in 1871. It is reprinted here in full, again, with minor edits.

AMONG the many beautiful homes destroyed in the North Division of the city, few, if any, were at once more elegant and home-like than that of the Hon. Isaac N. Arnold, the friend and biographer of Lincoln. The house was a large, plain, brick mansion, occupying with its grounds the whole block bounded by Erie, Huron, Pine, and Rush Streets. The grounds were filled with the most beautiful shrubbery and trees, and entirely secluded by a very luxuriant lilac hedge. Perhaps the most noticeable feature was the vines of wild grape, Virginia creeper, and bittersweet, which hung in graceful festoons from the massive elms, and covered with their dense foliage piazzas and summerhouses. There was a simple but quaint fountain, playing in front, beneath a perfect bower of overhanging vines. A great rock, upon which had been rudely carved the features of an Indian chief, had been pierced, and through this, a way had been made for the water, and over the head of the old chief the water of Lake Michigan was always throwing its spray. On one side of the entrance was a little greenhouse, always gay with flowers. Two vineries of choice varieties of foreign grapes, and a large greenhouse and barn, constituted the outbuildings. On the lawn was a sundial with the inscription:

"Horas non numero nisi serenas." (I number none but sunny hours.)

Alas! The tablet vindicated its motto but too well. It was broken by the heat or in the melee, which accompanied the fire, and the dark hours, which have followed, pass by without its reckoning.

99

But pleasant as was the outside, it was the interior wherein its great attractions lay; and the chief of these was the library. Here were the collections of the lifetime of a man of taste, wealth, and culture—a law library and a miscellaneous library of seven or eight thousand volumes. Many of the books were specialties, and the objects of pride and affection. Among them were the speeches of Burke, Sheridan, Fox, Pitt, Erskine, Curran, Brougham, Webster, Wirt, Seward, Sumner, etc., all superbly bound; a pretty full collection of English literature and history; the Abbotsford edition of Scott's novels, in full Russia binding; Pickering and Bacon, in tree calf; a full set of the British poets; all of Bonn's libraries, etc. In American literature and history the library was rich, including beautiful editions of the works of Cooper, Irving, Paulding, Willis, Bryant, Longfellow, Prescott, Holmes, the writings of Washington, Madison, Jefferson, Hamilton, Marshall, Story, Bancroft, and others.

Mr. Arnold had a very complete collection of the proceedings of Congress and the debates, from the organization of the Government down to the present day. In his library also was perhaps as full a collection of the books and pamphlets in relation to slavery, the rebellion, the war, and President Lincoln, as existed in any private hands. He had also ten large volumes of manuscript letters, written by distinguished military and civil characters during and since the war of the rebellion, including many from Lincoln, McClellan, Grant, Farragut, Sherman, Halleck, Seward, Sumner, Chase, Colfax, and others, of great personal and historic interest.

For the last ten years, Mr. Arnold had been collecting the speeches, writings, and letters of Lincoln for publication, and had many volumes of manuscripts and letters, the material for a strictly biographical work upon Abraham Lincoln, several chapters of which were ready for publication. These, with many rare and curious relics, prints, and engravings, have all perished.

100

The pictures were not numerous, but of very decided merit. There were landscapes by Kensett, Brown, and Mignot; family portraits by Healy; the original study of Webster's reply to Hayne, now in Faneuil Hall, Boston, in which were forty portraits of distinguished Americans, many of them from life; a portrait of Webster, by Chester Harding, etc.

The failure of Mr. Arnold to save anything, was the result of a most determined effort to save everything, and his too confident belief that he could succeed. Nor did this confidence seem to be unreasonable. His house, standing in the center of an open block, with a wide street and the Newberry block, with only one house, in front, and the Ogden block, with only one house, to the right, directly in the pathway of the flames, it is not surprising that he believed he could save his house. Besides, he had connections by hose with hydrants, both in front and rear of his house. Mrs. Arnold had placed what proved a better estimate upon the danger; and, calling up the family, and dressing little Alice, a child of eight years, she left the house and went to her daughter's (Mrs. Scudder), leaving Mr. A. and the remainder of the family— consisting of an older daughter, a lad of thirteen, a school-girl of fifteen, and the servants—to fight the battle with the flames. There was a sea of fire to the south and south-west; the wind blew a perfect gale, carrying smoke and sparks, shingles, pieces of lumber and roof, directly over the house. Everything was parched and dry as tinder. The leaves from the trees and shrubbery covered the ground. Mr. A. turned on the water to the fountains, to wet the ground and grass, and attached the hose to the hydrants. He stationed the servants on each side of the house, and others on the piazzas and for an hour and a half—perhaps two hours—was able, by the utmost vigilance and exertion, to extinguish the flames as often as they caught. During all this time, the fire was falling in torrents. There was literally a rain of fire. It

101

caught in the dry leaves; it caught in the grass, in the barn, in the piazzas, and as often as it caught it was extinguished before it got any headway. "When the barn first caught, the horses and the cow were removed to the lawn. The fight was successfully maintained until three o'clock in the morning. Every moment flakes of fire, falling upon dry wood, would be kindled by the high wind into a rapid blaze, and the next instant they would be extinguished. Every moment the contest grew warmer and more desperate, until, by three o'clock, the defenders of the castle were becoming seriously exhausted. At the hour mentioned, young Arthur Arnold called to his father, "The barn and hay are on fire!" "The leaves are on fire on the east side!" said the gardener. "The front piazza is in a blaze!" cried another. "The front greenhouse is in flames!" "The roof is on fire!" "The water has stopped!" was the last appalling announcement. "Now, for the first time," said Mr. A., " I gave up all hope of saving my home, and considered whether we could save any of its contents. My pictures, papers, and books—could I save them?"

An effort was made to cut down some portraits—a landscape of Kensett-Otsego Lake, by Mignot—it was too late! Seizing a bundle of papers, Mr. Arnold gathered the children and servants together, and, leading the terrified animals, they went forth from their so dearly cherished home. But whither? They were surrounded by fire on three sides; to the south, west, and north raged the flames, making a wall of fire and smoke from the ground to the sky. Their only escape was eastward to the lakeshore. Still leading the horses and cow, they went onward to the beach. Here were gathered thousands of fugitives, hemmed in and imprisoned by the raging element. The Sands, from the Government Pier north to Lill's Pier, a distance of three quarters of a mile, were covered with men, women, and children—some half-clad, in every variety of dress, with the motley collection of effects which they

102

sought to save. Some had silver, some valuable papers, some pictures, carpets, beds, etc. One little child had her doll tenderly pressed in her arms; an old Irish woman was cherishing a grunting pig; a fat woman had two large pillows, as portly as herself. There was a singular mixture of the awful, the ludicrous, and the pathetic.

Reaching the water's edge, Mr. A. says he paused to examine the situation and determine where was the least danger. Southwest, toward the river, were millions of feet of lumber, many shanties and wooden structures yet unburned, but which must be consumed before there could be any abatement of the danger. The air was full of cinders and smoke; the wind blew the heated sand worse than any sirocco. Where was a place of refuge? W. B. Ogden had lately constructed a long pier north of and parallel with the old United States pier, which prolongs the left bank of the river out into the lake, and this had been filled with stone, but had not been planked over; hence it would not readily burn. It was a hard road to travel, but it seemed the safest place, and Mr. Arnold and his children worked their way far out upon this pier. With much difficulty, the party crossed from the Ogden slip in a small rowboat and entered the lighthouse, where they, with Judge Goodrich, Mr. E. I. Tinkham, and others, were hospitably received.

The party remained prisoners in the lighthouse and on the pier on which it stood for several hours. The shipping in the river above was burning, the immense grain elevators of the Illinois Central and Northwestern Railroads were a mass of flames, and the pier itself, some distance up the river, was slowly burning toward the lighthouse. A large propeller, fastened to the dock a short distance up the river, took fire and burned. The danger was that as soon as the hawsers by which it was moored should be burned off, it would float down stream and set fire to the dock in the immediate vicinity of the lighthouse. Several propellers moved down near the mouth of the river, and took on board several hundred fugitives and steamed out into the lake. If the burning propeller should come down it would set fire to the pier, the lighthouse, and vast piles of lumber, which had escaped in consequence of being directly on shore and detached from the burning mass. A fire company was organized of those on the pier, and with water dipped in pails from the river, the fire was kept at bay. But all felt relieved when the propeller went to the bottom. The party were still prisoners on an angle of sand, and the fire running along the north shore of the river. The river and the fire prevented an escape to the south. West and north, the flames were still raging with unabated fury. The party waited for hours, hoping the fire would subside. The day wore on—noon passed—one, two o'clock, and still it seemed impossible to escape to land. Mr. Arnold, scouting to the northward, found his gardener right where he had left him, sitting upon the horse, far out in the lake, and holding on faithfully to the pony by its halter and to the cow by her horns. The escape to the north was pronounced impracticable for the ladies. And all the while they were in great danger and great anxiety concerning the fate of the missing mother and child.

Between three and four o'clock P. M., the tug "Clifford" steamed down the river, having escaped from the burning district, and tied up to the dock near the light-house. Could she return, taking the party up the river, through and beyond the fire to the west side? The captain thought he could. The bridges at Rush, State, Clark, and Wells Streets had all burned, and their fragments had fallen into the river. The great warehouses, stores, elevators, and docks along the river were still burning, but the fury of the fire had exhausted itself. The party determined to go through this narrow channel—to run the gauntlet of the fire to a point outside of the burnt district. This was the most dangerous experience of the day. The tug might take fire herself—her woodwork had been blistered by the heat as she came down. The engine might become unmanageable after she got inside the line of fire; or she might get entangled in the floating timbers and debris of the fallen bridges. However, the party determined to make the attempt. A full head of steam was gotten up; the hose was attached to the pumps, so that if the boat or the clothes of its passengers took fire they could be readily put out. The ladies and children were placed in the pilothouse, the windows shut, and the boat started—the men crouching close to the deck in the shelter of the bulwarks. At the State Street Bridge, the pilot had to pick his way very carefully through a mass of debris, and the situation began to look exceedingly hazardous. But it was too late to turn back, and so the voyagers pushed on, shooting as rapidly as possible past the hottest places, and slowing where the danger was from below. As they were passing State Street Bridge the pumps gave out, and they now ran great risk from fire. Arthur's hat blew away, and his father covered his face and head with a handkerchief, which he had dipped in the water. Finally, they passed the Wells Street Bridge, and were still unscathed.

"Is not the worst over?" asked Mr. Arnold of the captain.

"We are through, sir," was the answer.

"We are safe, thank God!" came from hearts and lips, as the boat emerged from the smoke into the clear, cool air outside the fire lines.

Search for the missing ones was immediately commenced. Mr. Arnold spent over twenty-four hours in driving and wandering in pursuit of his wife—now passing among the throng of refugees at Lincoln Park and peering into every grimy countenance—now getting a clue, whether true or false, and dashing off by a train into a suburb—now baffled entirely and compelled to commence the search entirely anew. Sometime during the following afternoon his efforts were rewarded by learning that his wife and child were at the house of Judge Drummond, of the U. S. Circuit Court, at a suburb called Winfield; and there, during the evening of Tuesday, the family were reunited and joined in thanks to God for their mutual deliverance.

We have given this sketch of a single family's experience in this terrible ordeal, not because it is more thrilling than that of thousands of other families, but rather because it is a specimen of the whole, and because Mr. Arnold is well known in the West. There were many homes in the North Division which, like this one, were noted for their exclusive elegance— their aristocratic seclusion, one might say—and which gave the inhabitants of this quarter a just pride in their locality. The three residences mentioned in the present chapter—the Newberry, the Ogden (Wm. B.), and the Arnold places, with the famous McCagg place, on North Clark Street, and one or two others, occupied territory which alone was worth at least. a quarter of a million to each place, and this gave the proprietors some such prima facie title to aristocracy as landed estates do to their owners in England. They indicated at once that the occupant must possess a mine of wealth in the form of stores over-town, in order to maintain such homesteads in the face of constant offers of hundreds of dollars per foot of their street front. But they are all gone now, stores and giant elms together! Mr. McCagg, who was away in Europe at the time, lost, besides his mansion and its contents, which included many precious paintings and a library of rare works, one of his greenhouses, the finest in the West. Mr. Perry H. Smith, the well-known railroad manager and capitalist, lost a library valued at $50,000, and noted for the superb bindings of its volumes, many of which Mr. Smith had but just brought from Europe.

Part Thirteen
Chief Marshal Williams

THE LOST CITY!

DRAMA OF THE FIRE-FIEND'

—OR—

CHICAGO,

AS IT WAS, AND AS IT IS!

AND ITS

Glorious Future!

A VIVID AND TRUTHFUL PICTURE OF ALL OF INTEREST CON-
NECTED WITH THE DESTRUCTION OF CHICAGO AND
THE TERRIBLE FIRES OF THE
GREAT NORTH-WEST.

STARTLING, THRILLING INCIDENTS,

FRIGHTFUL SCENES, HAIR-BREADTH ESCAPES, INDIVIDUAL
HEROISM, SELF-SACRIFICES, PERSONAL ANECDOTES,
&c., TOGETHER WITH A HISTORY OF CHICAGO
FROM ITS ORIGIN, STATISTICS OF THE
GREAT FIRES OF THE WORLD, &c.

BY FRANK LUZERNE,

A RESIDENT OF CHICAGO FOR TWENTY-FIVE YEARS, AND AN EYE WITNESS OF THE TERRIBLE
CONFLAGRATION.

EDITED BY JOHN G. WELLS,

AUTHOR OF WELLS' EVERY MAN HIS OWN LAWYER; WELLS' ILLUSTRATED NATIONAL HAND-BOOK;
AND OTHER POPULAR WORKS.

———

PROFUSELY ILLUSTRATED WITH MAPS AND ENGRAVINGS FROM PHOTOGRAPHS TAKEN ON THE SPOT.

———

New York:

WELLS & COMPANY, 432 BROOME STREET.
M. A. PARKER & CO., 152 SOUTH MORGAN ST., CHICAGO, ILLS.
B. R. STURGES, 81 WASHINGTON ST., BOSTON, MASS.
A. L. BANCROFT & CO., SAN FRANCISCO, CALIFORNIA.

1872.

108

A reporter's interview with Chicago Fire Department's Chief Marshal Robert A. Williams as it appeared in *The Lost City, Drama of the Fire Fiend or Chicago, As It Was, and As It Is!* by Frank Luzerne.

THE FIRE MARSHAL'S GRAPHIC STORY OF THE GREAT FIRE.

STARTLING INCIDENTS FORCIBLY DETAILED.

A reporter for the daily press called upon the Fire Marshal for his version of certain matters connected with the fire, and obtained, in a few pointed words, the best history of some of the most startling events yet given to the public. We are indebted to the Chicago Evening Mail for the following graphic "interview" which will be found intensely interesting, and more exciting than any other account occupying double the amount of space:

Reporter.—Some of our exchanges have hinted that members of the Fire Department were drunk during the fire, and I have called on you, as one who had the best opportunity of knowing, to have the facts in the case.

Marshal.—Well, sir, I don't know how it was elsewhere, but I did not see a drunken fireman that night.

Reporter.—What is the character of the firemen in this respect?

Marshal.—They are a tolerable steady set when on duty.

Reporter.—Who appoints them?

Marshal.—The Board of Police. I have not had the opportunity of choosing a single one of my men.

Reporter.—What may have given rise to the report of drunkenness?

Marshal.—I don't know exactly, but I did see a drunken bummer with a fireman's hat on, and I took it away from him. He begged me to let him keep it, but I refused to. I took it to the engineer of No 6 and told him to take care of it, and it wasn't long before I saw another fireman's hat walking off with a drunken fellow under it, and I took it away from him also. It may have been that others saw these two thieves and swore that the firemen were drunk.

Reporter.—Very likely; but these witnesses say they saw the firemen working at the engines, and that they were staggering.

Marshal—But bless your soul (and here the Marshal got interesting, not to say excited, and raised up on his elbow and threatened the reporter's nose with his finger) the heat was awful; 'twas like hell, and the firemen's eyes were red with the dust and fire, so that many of them were most blind. The hair was scorched off their faces, and they stuck to their machines like bulldogs, and worked them till they couldn't stand it any longer. Yes, sir, and they did stagger, for they were clean beat, and many of them, had to go home for the exhaustion from the heat. They were tired, too, from the fire of the night before, and then to give the same men such a long pull again, why, an iron man couldn't have stood it.

Reporter.—I hear the firemen were demoralized.

Marshal.—Well, now, it is pretty hard work for flesh and nerves to gain a victory, and then have to go to work again, and again, and again, and fight it all over. But that is just what the men did. And after they heard the waterworks were burned down they didn't give up; and they never quit working till all the water in the reservoirs

110

and mains was used up. I don't think that was being demoralized; not much.

Reporter.—How was it that they got the victory? It looks to me as if it was a defeat worse than Waterloo.

Marshal.—'Twas water low, that was what hindered us from saving a large part of the North Division. But I tell you we got the fire under; and if it hadn't been for that awful gale, we would have been all right.

When I got down to the fire Sunday night, I got the engines all around it, and had hemmed it in so that it wouldn't have lived very much longer, when one of the men came and said, there is a church on fire north of us ;and, sure enough, there was a church steeple all in a blaze two squares off, so I sent down an engine and pretty soon got two more to work on it, and had saved the long line of cottages just east of it, and the drug store across the road, and though the heat was awful, we had got it right under our thumb, when someone told us that the fire had caught still farther north. So I went down and there was the match factory just blazing, and the brick factory was smoking, and Bateham's shingle mills' yard was covered with shavings and cinders and flakes and flashing boards, just raining down on it so that it was on fire in more than a dozen places at once, and just beyond was the hardwood lumber yard, and everything dry as a bone, and as greedy to burn as gun-powder.

I hadn't more than got this surrounded when the Canal street people had kindled a new fire right in the middle of the street, though they didn't mean to, for they had piled up beds and bedding and furniture in the street, and it took fire and then it went away like feathers, for the wind would take up a blazing

111

mattress and fling it against a house, and that house went right down before you could get there. But I was just thinking that we would run the fire into the burnt district and stop it there, when they told me the fire was on the South Side. So I told the Fred Gund to get out of that right away, as the fire was coming awful heavy on her, and went across to Conley's Patch. The fire had then got well started, in two small buildings south of the Armory, and it just tore up Wells street, under those houses set on posts, and sidewalks raised up from the streets. Then I saw we should have heavy work before us.

Vandercook wanted some powder, but I told him we had none, and he went off to get some.

I had just got two engines to work when Jack said: "My God, she's ahead of us." So we went down, and you remember that carpenter shop behind the Oriental building and them low wooden sheds? Well, sir, they were blazing. I ordered up the Chicago and broke out the glass in the lower front window (that's where I got my hand hurt, you see,) and took the hose right through the basement, but the flames drove us out, and it wasn't long before the Oriental Hall was just rolling in flames. Why, if that building had iron shutters on her, she wouldn't have burned; but the wind was fearful now. I saw a blazing board go right through the back window of a building in the block facing north on Washington, and pretty soon it was blazing fearful.

BLOWING UP.

Vandercook then came with the powder, and put it in the basement of the Union Bank building, but it just puffed and never jarred the block a bit, and before they could get ready to give her another lift, they could not live inside of her. You see I thought we

112

could save Sheridan's headquarters if we could only blow down the block across the street, but it was too late. Just then, the Court House took fire, and I sent an engine to the Sherman House, hoping to save that, for I thought that the tower of the Court House would fall inside, and with the wide-open space, we should have some chance left yet. But the wind was just tremendous. I saw it blow a man against the lamppost at the Pittsburgh and Fort Wayne ticket office, across the street from the Sherman House, and the post and the man came down together. A. H. Miller's store caught fire in six places from the awnings rolled up, and they served as pockets for the fire to lodge in. Then the old Tribune building got on fire, but I hoped yet to save the Sherman, when I found that those old wooden buildings on the south side of Lake street, and the sheds just south of them were just roaring with flame. Why the fire just roared like a lion, and I saw the Sherman House was gone up. Then I thought of my family in Thompson & Templeton's block, and I found that my wife had got all ready to go; but before we could get out anything but the piano and one chair, the house was too hot to hold us.

Just then, someone said the Water Works were on fire. R. B. Crane said he didn't believe it. So he drove up with a horse and buggy, and he says before he got there the flames were coming out of all the windows. It caught from some cinders from the Court House or the Board of Trade. (They say cinders were on the crib, but I don't believe that, interrupted the reporter). Yes, sir, they were, and if you go out there you will see the marks on the roof, and it was life or death with the keeper and his wife, and they pumped water and put out the sparks, or the crib and they too would have gone, and perhaps you won't believe it, but a man was plowing up at Evanston, and that's 10 or 12 miles, and he saw sparks falling all around him; oh, you have no idea how the wind

113

blew that night, and then there was something, I think, I don't know, I shouldn't like exactly to say it, but there must have been fire below ground as well as in the wind overhead. Two strangers came to me the next day and said they were strangers from the East stopping at the Sherman House, and when they saw that was going they went to the next street, and while standing there they saw a blue flame coming up through the iron gratings at the corner, and on looking in saw the whole basement on fire, and not a spark in the rest of the building. You saw at the corner of Wells and Randolph the road hove up; well, I followed that down to the gas-works, and it was raised up in half a dozen places; that was where the gas took fire and burst in the sewers. When the gas-works took fire, they let off the gas into the sewers, and the enormous gasometer fell down to the ground; and I think perhaps the buildings were filled with gas from the sewers and private drains, and took fire inside as well as from the roof overhead. People seemed stupified and crazed, and instead of putting out the sparks on their roofs, just let them burn, and the wind would take up pieces of blazing felt as big as half a sheet, and carry it up to a wooden cornice, and then that building was gone. And I didn't know but Allen was helping us on the West Side, when he and ten or twelve more were cut off, and they made up their mind they would have to swim for life. Allen had just stripped to his shirt and drawers when a tug and two vessels came along and took them aboard; and while they held up long enough for that, the masts and rigging of the boats took fire. The tug cast them off below Van Buren Street Bridge and put Allen and his crowd ashore. Here Allen saw a fire on Quincy street, and says that if the houses had been covered with kerosene they could not have burned so fast while he was going only two squares. So, with everything making against us, no wonder we couldn't get ahead.

114

Reporter.—But had you engines enough?

Marshall.—All the engines ever made couldn't stop her at the Oriental Building. She kept a jumping over our heads all the time so we couldn't get ahead. We had only fifteen engines in all. Two were at the repair shop, and only one engine was burned, for we saved all of the engines that were being repaired.

Boston has 21 engines, but she hasn't half the territory; and look at her buildings. New York has twice as many as we, compared with her size. I wanted the Board to let me have six floating engines last year, but they wouldn't, and if we'd had them the night of the fire we could have saved the elevators, for the fire crowded us so that we couldn't work but a mighty little while till we had to move. One of our engines didn't have time to unscrew her coupling, so they took an axe and broke down the hydrant and took it along with them, and even then the hair was singed off the horses.

This account reads like the veriest romance, and yet there is no question of its correctness, for the Marshal is not only a man of known integrity, but his account is authenticated from the mouths of scores of witnesses, equally reliable and wholly disinterested.

THROUGH THE FLAMES AND BEYOND, OR CHICAGO AS IT WAS AND AS IT IS.

WELLS & CO

Part Fourteen
Bibliography

_____. *The Great Fire of Chicago.* Indianapolis: S.E. Tilford, 1871

Andreas, A.T. *A History of Chicago.* New York:1884-1886

Angle, Paul M. *The Great Chicago Fire.* Chicago: University of Chicago Press, 1946

Bales, Richard F. *The Great Chicago Fire and The Myth of Mrs. O'Leary's Cow.* Jefferson, NC: McFarland & Company, Inc., 2002

Barclay, George Lippard. *The Great Fire of Chicago.* Philadelphia: Barclay & Co., 1872

Blatchford M.E. and W.E. *Memories of the Chicago Fire.* Chicago: Mr. and Mrs. Paul Blatchford, 1921

Colbert, Elias, and Chamberlin, Everett. *Chicago and the Great Conflagration.* Cincinnati and New York: C.F. Vent, 1871

Cromie, Robert. *The Great Chicago Fire.* Nashville: Rutledge Hill Press, 1994

Gerty, Francis J. Editor. *October 9, 1871 The Burning of Chicago.* Chicago: The Hendricks School Press, 1915

Kogan, Herman, and Lloyd Wendt. *Chicago: A Pictorial History.* New York: Dutton, 1958

Lowe, David Garrard, Editor. *The Great Chicago Fire.* Mineola, New York: Dover Publications, Inc., 1979

Luzerne, Frank. *The Lost City, Drama of the Fire Fiend or Chicago, As It Was, and As It Is and Its Glorious Future.* New York: Harper and Sons, 1872

Miller, Donald L. *City of the Century.* New York: Simon & Schuster, 1996

Murphy, Jim. *The Great Fire.* New York: Scholastic, 1995

Pendleton, William E., and Hart, Richard T. *Recollections of a Bygone Era.* New York: Cassell Petter & Galpin, 1896

Sawislak, Karen. *Smoldering City.* Chicago: University of Chicago Press, 1995

Sewell, Alfred L. *The Great Calamity.* Chicago: Alfred L. Sewell, 1871

Additional books by William Pack

The Essential Houdini

The Essential P.T. Barnum

The Discovery of Magic

The Essential Great Chicago Fire

Available through williampack.com

"If you want to watch a group of adults mesmerized at an event, invite William. Three weeks later, those who attended still comment on the program. William captivated us with his stories. He brings energy, wit, and fascinating props and illustrations to a terrific program that will stay with you and your patrons. He engages the audience at every step of the program, entertains and educates with a twinkle in his eye."
-Elke Saylor Muskego Library, WI

William is available for shows and performance lectures custom suited for your event. For more information, please visit williampack.com

To contact William,
email: bill@williampack.com

57752946R00077

Made in the USA
Charleston, SC
24 June 2016